THE SUNSHINE BOYS

THE SUNSHINE BOYS

A New Comedy by

NEIL SIMON

RANDOM HOUSE
NEW YORK

To John . . . who brought the light to all of us.

THE SUNSHINE BOYS *was first presented on December 20, 1972, by Emanuel Azenberg and Eugene V. Wolsk at the Broadhurst Theatre, New York City, with the following cast:*

(In order of appearance)

WILLIE CLARK	Jack Albertson
BEN SILVERMAN	Lewis J. Stadlen
AL LEWIS	Sam Levene
PATIENT	Joe Young
EDDIE	John Batiste
NURSE	Lee Meredith
REGISTERED NURSE	Minnie Gentry

Directed by	Alan Arkin
Scenery by	Kert Lundell
Costumes by	Albert Wolsky
Lighting by	Tharon Musser

The Scene

The action takes place in New York City.

Act One

SCENE ONE: A small apartment in an old hotel on upper Broadway, in the mid-Eighties. It is an early afternoon in midwinter.

SCENE TWO: The following Monday, late morning.

Act Two

SCENE ONE: A Manhattan television studio.

SCENE TWO: The same as Act One. It is two weeks later, late afternoon.

ACT
ONE

The scene is a two-room apartment in an old hotel on upper Broadway, in the mid-Eighties. It's rather a depressing place. There is a bed, a bureau, a small dining table with two chairs, an old leather chair that faces a TV set on a cheap, metal stand. There is a small kitchen to one side—partitioned off from the living room by a curtain—a small bathroom on the other. A window looks out over Broadway. It is early afternoon, midwinter.

At rise, the TV is on, and the banal dialogue of a soap opera drones on. In the leather chair sits WILLIE CLARK, *in slippers, pajamas and an old bathrobe.* WILLIE *is in his seventies. He watches the program but is constantly dozing off, then catching himself and watching for a few more minutes at a time. The set drones on and* WILLIE *dozes off. The tea kettle on the stove in the kitchen comes to a boil and whistles.* WILLIE'S *head perks up at the sound; he reaches over and picks up the telephone.*

WILLIE *(Into the phone)* Hello? . . . Who's this?
(The whistle continues from the kettle, and WILLIE *looks over in that direction. He bangs up the phone and does not seem embarrassed or even aware of his own absentmindedness. He simply crosses into the kitchen and turns off the flame under the kettle)*

3

VOICE FROM TV   We'll be back with *Storm Warning* after this brief message from Lipton Tea.

WILLIE   Don't worry, I'm not going anywhere.
(He puts a tea ball into a mug and pours the boiling water in. Then he goes over to the dining table in the living room, takes a spoon, dips into a jar of honey, and pours it into his tea. He glances over at the TV set, which has just played the Lipton Tea commercial)

VOICE FROM TV   And now for Part Three of today's *Storm Warning . . .*

WILLIE   What happened to Part Two? I missed Part Two? *(He drinks his tea as Part Three continues and the banal dialogue drones on. WILLIE listens as he shuffles toward his chair. The TV set, which is away from the wall, has an electric plug running from it, along the ground and into the wall. WILLIE, who never seems to look where he's going, comes up against the cord with his foot, inadvertently pulling the cord out of its socket in the wall. The TV set immediately dies. WILLIE sits, then looks at the set. Obviously, no picture. He gets up and fiddles with the dials. How could his best friend desert him at a time like this? He hits the set on the top with his hand)* What's the matter with you? *(He hits the set again and twists the knobs futilely, never thinking for a moment it might be something as simple as the plug. He slaps the picture tube)* Come on, for Pete's sakes, what are you doing there? *(He stares at it in disbelief. He kicks the stand on which it rests. Then he crosses to the phone, and picks it up)* Hello? . . . Sandy? . . . Let me have Sandy . . . Sandy? . . . My television's dead . . . My television . . . Is this Sandy? . . . My television died . . . No, not Willie. Mr. Clark to you, please . . . Never

4

mind the jokes, wise guy, it's not funny . . . Send up somebody to fix my dead television . . . I didn't touch nothing . . . Nothing, I'm telling you . . . It's a crappy set . . . You live in a crappy hotel, you get a crappy television . . . The what? . . . The plug? . . . What plug? . . . Wait a minute. *(He lays the phone down, crosses to behind the set, bends down, picks up the plug and looks at it. He goes back to the telephone. Into the phone)* Hello? . . . It's not the plug. It's something else. I'll fix it myself. *(He hangs up, goes over to the wall plug and plugs it in. The set goes back on)* He tells me the plug . . . When he calls me Mr. Clark then I'll tell him it was the plug. *(He sits and picks up his cup of tea)* The hell with all of 'em. *(There is a knock on the door.* WILLIE *looks at the wall on the opposite side of the room)* Bang all you want, I'm not turning it off. I'm lucky it works.

> *(There is a pause; then a knock on the front door again, this time accompanied by a male voice)*

BEN'S VOICE   Uncle Willie? It's me. Ben.
> *(*WILLIE *turns and looks at the front door, not acknowledging that he was mistaken about the knocking on the other wall)*

WILLIE   Who's that?

BEN'S VOICE   Ben.

WILLIE   Ben? Is that you?

BEN'S VOICE   Yes, Uncle Willie, it's Ben. Open the door.

WILLIE   Wait a minute. *(He rises, crosses to the door, tripping over the TV cord again, disconnecting the set. He starts to unlatch the door, but has trouble manipulating it. His fingers are not too manipulative)* Wait a minute . . . (*He is having great difficulty with it*) . . . Wait a minute.

BEN'S VOICE   Is anything wrong?

WILLIE (*Still trying*)   Wait a minute.
  (*He tries forcing it*)

BEN'S VOICE   What's the matter?

WILLIE   I'm locked in. The lock is broken, I'm locked in. Go down and tell the boy. Sandy. Tell Sandy that Mr. Clark is locked in.

BEN'S VOICE   What is it, the latch?

WILLIE   It's the latch. It's broken, I'm locked in. Go tell the boy Sandy, they'll get somebody.

BEN'S VOICE   That happened last week. Don't try to force it. Just slide it out. (WILLIE *stares at the latch*) Uncle Willie, do you hear me? Don't force it. Slide it out.

WILLIE (*Fiddling with the latch*)   Wait a minute. (*Carefully, he slides it open*) It's open. Never mind, I did it myself.
  (*He opens the door.* BEN SILVERMAN, *a well dressed man in his early thirties, enters. He is wearing a topcoat and carrying a shopping bag from Bloomingdale's, filled to the brim with assorted foodstuffs and a copy of the weekly* Variety)

BEN   You probably have to oil it.

6

WILLIE I don't have to oil nothing. The hell with 'em.
(BEN *hangs up his coat in the closet*)

BEN (*Crosses to the table with the shopping bag*) You feeling all right?

WILLIE What is this, Wednesday?

BEN (*Puzzled*) Certainly. Don't I always come on Wednesdays?

WILLIE But this is Wednesday today?

BEN (*Puts his bag down*) Yes, of course. Haven't you been out?

WILLIE When?

BEN Today. Yesterday. This week. You haven't been out all week?

WILLIE (*Crossing to him*) Sunday. I was out Sunday. I went to the park Sunday.
(BEN *hands* WILLIE *the* Variety. WILLIE *tucks it under his arm and starts to look through the shopping bag*)

BEN What are you looking for?

WILLIE (*Going through the bag*) My *Variety*.

BEN I just gave it to you. It's under your arm.

WILLIE (*Looks under his arm*) Why do you put it there? He puts it under my arm.

BEN (*Starts taking items out of the bag*) Have you been eating properly? No corned beef sandwiches, I hope.

7

WILLIE (*Opens to the back section*) Is this today's?

BEN Certainly it's today's. *Variety* comes out on Wednesday, doesn't it? And today is Wednesday.

WILLIE I'm just asking, don't get so excited. (BEN *shakes his head in consternation*) . . . Because I already read last Wednesday's.

BEN (*Takes more items out*) I got you six different kinds of soups. All low-sodium, salt-free. All very good for you . . . Are you listening?

WILLIE (*His head in the paper*) I'm listening. You got six lousy-tasting soups . . . Did you see this?

BEN What?

WILLIE What I'm looking at. Did you see this?

BEN How do I know what you're looking at?

WILLIE Two new musicals went into rehearsals today and I didn't even get an audition. Why didn't I get an audition?

BEN Because there were no parts for you. One of them is a young rock musical and the other show is all black.

WILLIE What's the matter, I can't do black? I did black in 1928. And when I did black, you understood the words, not like today.

BEN I'm sorry, you're not the kind of black they're looking for. (*He shivers*) Geez, it's cold in here. You know it's freezing in here? Don't they ever send up any heat?

WILLIE (*Has turned a page*) How do you like that? Sol Burton died.

BEN Who?

WILLIE Sol Burton. The songwriter. Eighty-nine years old, went like that, from nothing.

BEN Why didn't you put on a sweater?

WILLIE I knew him very well . . . A terrible person. Mean, mean. He should rest in peace, but he was a mean person. His best friends didn't like him.

BEN *(Goes to the bureau for a sweater)* Why is it so cold in here?

WILLIE You know what kind of songs he wrote? . . . The worst. The worst songs ever written were written by Sol Burton. *(He sings)* "Lady, Lady, be my baby . . ." Did you ever hear anything so rotten? Baby he rhymes with lady . . . No wonder he's dead.
     (He turns the page)

BEN This radiator is ice-cold. Look, Uncle Willie, I'm not going to let you live here any more. You've got to let me find you another place . . . I've been asking you for seven years now. You're going to get sick.

WILLIE *(Still looking at* Variety*)* Tom Jones is gonna get a hundred thousand dollars a week in Las Vegas. When Lewis and I were headlining at the Palace, the *Palace* didn't cost a hundred thousand dollars.

BEN That was forty years ago. And forty years ago this hotel was twenty years old. They should tear it down. They take advantage of all you people in here because they know you don't want to move.
     (WILLIE crosses to the table and looks into the shopping bag)

9

WILLIE   No cigars?

BEN   (*Making notes on his memo pad*)   You're not supposed to have cigars.

WILLIE   Where's the cigars?

BEN   You know the doctor told you you're not supposed
to smoke cigars any more. I didn't bring any.

WILLIE   Gimme the cigars.

BEN   What cigars? I just said I don't have them. Will you
forget the cigars?

WILLIE   Where are they, in the bag?

BEN   On the bottom. I just brought three. It's the last
time I'm doing it.

WILLIE   (*Takes out a bag with three cigars*)   How's your
family? The children all right?
     (*He removes one cigar*)

BEN   Suddenly you're interested in my family? It's not
going to work, Uncle Willie. I'm not bringing you any
more cigars.

WILLIE   I just want to know how the children are.

BEN   The children are fine. They're wonderful, thank
you.

WILLIE   Good. Next time bring the big cigars.
     (*He puts two cigars in the breast pocket of his bath-
robe and the other one in his mouth. He crosses into
the kitchen looking for a light*)

10

BEN You don't even know their names. What are the names of my children?

WILLIE Millie and Sidney.

BEN Amanda and Michael.

WILLIE What's the matter, you didn't like Millie and Sidney?

BEN I was *never* going to name them Millie and Sidney. You forgot, so you made something up. You forget everything. I'll bet you didn't drink the milk from last week. I'll bet it's still in the refrigerator. (*Crosses quickly, and opens the refrigerator and looks in*) There's the milk from last week.

WILLIE (*Comes out of the kitchen, still looking for a light*) Do they know who I am?

BEN (*Looking through the refrigerator*) Who?

WILLIE Amanda and Sidney.

BEN Amanda and Michael. That you were a big star in vaudeville? They're three years old, Uncle Willie, you think they remember vaudeville? *I* never saw vaudeville . . . This refrigerator won't last another two days.

WILLIE Did you tell them six times on *The Ed Sullivan Show?*
    (*He sits, tries a cigarette lighter. It's broken*)

BEN They never heard of Ed Sullivan. Uncle Willie, they're three years old. They don't follow show business. (*Comes back into the living room and sees* WILLIE *with the cigar in his mouth*) What are you doing? You're

11

not going to smoke that now. You promised me you'd only smoke one after dinner.

WILLIE Am I smoking it? Do you see smoke coming from the cigar?

BEN But you've got it in your mouth.

WILLIE I'm rehearsing . . . After dinner I'll do the show.

BEN (*Crossing back into the kitchen*) I'm in the most aggravating business in the whole world and I never get aggravated until I come here.
     (*He opens the cupboards and looks in*)

WILLIE (*Looking around*) So don't come. I got Social Security.

BEN You think that's funny? I don't think that's funny, Uncle Willie.

WILLIE (*Thumbing through* Variety) If you had a sense of humor, you'd think it was funny.

BEN (*Angrily, through gritted teeth*) I have a *terrific* sense of humor.

WILLIE Like your father—he laughed once in 1932.

BEN I can't talk to you.

WILLIE Why, they're funny today? Tell me who you think is funny today, and I'll show you where he's not funny.

BEN Let's not get into that, huh? I've got to get back to the office. Just promise me you'll have a decent lunch today.

WILLIE   If I were to tell a joke and got a laugh from you, I'd throw it out.

BEN   How can I laugh when I see you like this, Uncle Willie? You sit in your pajamas all day in a freezing apartment watching soap operas on a thirty-five-dollar television set that doesn't have a horizontal hold. The picture just keeps rolling from top to bottom—pretty soon your eyes are gonna roll around your head . . . You never eat anything. You never go out because you don't know how to work the lock on the door. Remember when you locked yourself in the bathroom overnight? It's a lucky thing you keep bread in there, you would have starved . . . And you wonder why I worry.

WILLIE   Calvin Coolidge, that's your kind of humor.

BEN   Look, Uncle Willie, promise me you'll eat decently.

WILLIE   I'll eat decently. I'll wear a blue suit, a white shirt and black shoes.

BEN   And if you're waiting for a laugh, you're not going to get one from me.

WILLIE   Who could live that long? Get me a job instead of a laugh.

BEN   (Sighs, exasperatedly)   You know I've been trying, Uncle Willie. It's not easy. There's not much in town. Most of the work is commercials and . . . well, you know, we've had a little trouble in that area.

WILLIE   The potato chips? The potato chips wasn't my fault.

BEN   Forget the potato chips.

13

WILLIE What about the Shick Injector? Didn't I audition funny on the Shick Injector?

BEN You were very funny but your hand was shaking. And you can't show a man shaving with a shaky hand.

WILLIE Why couldn't you get me on the Alka-Seltzer? That's my kind of comedy. I got a terrific face for an upset stomach.

BEN I've submitted you twenty times.

WILLIE What's the matter with twenty-one?

BEN Because the word is out in the business that you can't remember the lines, and they're simply not interested.

WILLIE *(That hurt)* I couldn't remember the lines? I COULDN'T REMEMBER THE LINES? I don't remember that.

BEN For the Frito-Lays potato chips. I sent you over to the studio, you couldn't even remember the address.

WILLIE Don't tell me I didn't remember the lines. The lines I remembered beautifully. The name of the potato chip I couldn't remember . . . What was it?

BEN Frito-Lays.

WILLIE Say it again.

BEN Frito-Lays.

WILLIE I still can't remember it—because it's not funny. If it's funny, I remember it. Alka-Seltzer is funny. You

14

say "Alka-Seltzer," you get a laugh. The other word is not funny. What is it?

BEN Frito-Lays.

WILLIE Maybe in *Mexico* that's funny, not here. Fifty-seven years I'm in this business, you learn a few things. You know what makes an audience laugh. Do you know which words are funny and which words are *not* funny?

BEN You told me a hundred times, Uncle Willie. Words with a "K" in it are funny.

WILLIE Words with a "K" in it are funny. You didn't know that, did you? If it doesn't have a "K," it's not funny. I'll tell you which words always get a laugh.
(He is about to count on his fingers)

BEN Chicken.

WILLIE Chicken is funny.

BEN Pickle.

WILLIE Pickle is funny.

BEN Cupcake.

WILLIE Cupcake is funny . . . Tomato is *not* funny. Roast beef is *not* funny.

BEN But cookie is funny.

WILLIE But cookie is funny.

BEN Uncle Willie, you've explained that to me ever since I was a little boy.

WILLIE Cucumber is funny.

BEN *(Falling in again)* Car keys.

WILLIE Car keys is funny.

BEN Cleveland.

WILLIE Cleveland is funny . . . Maryland is *not* funny.

BEN Listen, I have to get back to the office, Uncle Willie, but there's something I'd like to talk to you about first. I got a call yesterday from C.B.S.

WILLIE Casey Stengel, that's a funny name; Robert Taylor is not funny.

BEN *(Sighs exasperatedly)* Why don't you listen to me?

WILLIE I heard. You got a call from N.B.C.

BEN C.B.S.

WILLIE Whatever.

BEN C.B.S. is doing a big special next month. An hour and a half variety show. They're going to have some of the biggest names in the history of show business. They're trying to get Flip Wilson to host the show.

WILLIE Him I like. He gives me a laugh. With the dress and the little giggle and the red wig. That's a funny boy . . . What's the boy's name again?

BEN Flip Wilson. And it doesn't have a K.

WILLIE But he's *black*, with a "K." You see what I mean?

BEN *(Looks to heaven for help. It doesn't come)* I do, I do. The theme of this variety show—

16

WILLIE What's the theme of the show?

BEN *The theme of the show* is the history of comedy dating from the early Greek times, through the days of vaudeville, right up to today's stars.

WILLIE Why couldn't you get me on this show?

BEN I *got* you on the show.

WILLIE Alone?

BEN With Lewis.

WILLIE *(Turns away)* You ain't got me on the show.

BEN Let me finish.

WILLIE You're finished. It's no.

BEN Can't you wait until I'm through before you say "no"? Can't we discuss it for a minute?

WILLIE I'm busy.

BEN Doing what?

WILLIE Saying "no."

BEN You can have the courtesy of hearing me out. They begged me at C.B.S. *Begged* me.

WILLIE Talk faster, because you're coming up to another "no."

BEN They said to me the history of comedy in the United States would not be complete unless they included one of the greatest teams ever to come out of vaudeville,

Lewis and Clark, The Sunshine Boys. The vice-president of C.B.S. said this to me on the phone.

WILLIE The vice-president said this?

BEN Yes. He is the greatest Lewis and Clark fan in this country. He knows by heart every one of your old routines.

WILLIE Then let *him* go on with that bastard.

BEN It's one shot. You would just have to do it one night, one of the old sketches. They'll pay ten thousand dollars for the team. That's top money for these shows, I promise you. Five thousand dollars apiece. And that's more money than you've earned in two years.

WILLIE I don't need money. I live alone. I got two nice suits, I don't have a pussycat, I'm very happy.

BEN You're *not* happy. You're miserable.

WILLIE *I'm happy!* I just *look* miserable!

BEN You're dying to go to work again. You call me six times a day in the office. I can't see over my desk for all your messages.

WILLIE Call me back sometime, you won't get so many messages.

BEN I call you every day of the week. I'm up here every Wednesday, rain or shine, winter or summer, flu or diphtheria.

WILLIE What are you, a mailman? You're a nephew. I don't ask you to come. You're my brother's son, you've been very nice to me. I appreciate it, but I've never asked you for anything . . . except for a job. You're a good boy but a stinking agent.

BEN   I'M A GOOD AGENT? Damn it, don't say that to me, Uncle Willie, I'm a *goddamn good agent!*

WILLIE   What are you screaming for? What is it, such a wonderful thing to be a good agent?

BEN   *(Holds his chest)*   I'm getting chest pains. You give me chest pains, Uncle Willie.

WILLIE   It's *my* fault you get excited?

BEN   Yes, it's *your* fault! I only get chest pains on Wednesdays.

WILLIE   So come on Tuesdays.

BEN   *(Starts for the door)*   I'm going. I don't even want to discuss this with you any more. You're impossible to talk to. FORGET THE VARIETY SHOW!
     (He starts for the door)

WILLIE   I forgot it.

BEN   *(Stops)*   I'm not coming back any more. I'm not bringing you your *Variety* or your cigars or your low-sodium soups—do you understand, Uncle Willie? I'm not bringing you anything any more.

WILLIE   Good. Take care of yourself. Say hello to Millie and Phyllis.

BEN   I'm not asking you to be partners again. If you two don't get along, all right. But this is just for one night. One last show. Once you get an exposure like that,

Alka-Seltzer will come begging to *me* to sign you up. Jesus, how is it going to look if I go back to the office and tell them I couldn't make a deal with my own uncle?

WILLIE   My personal opinion? Lousy!

BEN *(Falls into a chair, exhausted)*   Do you really hate Al Lewis that much?

WILLIE *(Looks away)*   I don't discuss Al Lewis any more.

BEN *(Gets up)*   We *have* to discuss him, because C.B.S. is waiting for an answer today, and if we turn them down, I want to have a pretty good reason why. You haven't seen him in—what? ten years now.

WILLIE   *(Takes a long time before answering)*   Eleven years!

BEN *(Amazed)*   You mean to tell me you haven't spoken to him in eleven years?

WILLIE   I haven't *seen* him in eleven years. I haven't *spoken* to him in twelve years.

BEN   You mean you saw him for a whole year that you didn't speak to him?

WILLIE   It wasn't easy. I had to sneak around backstage a lot.

BEN   But you spoke to him onstage.

WILLIE   Not to *him*. If he played a gypsy, I spoke to the gypsy. If he played a lunatic, I spoke to the lunatic. But that bastard I didn't speak to.

BEN   I can't believe that.

WILLIE You don't believe it? I can show you witnesses who *saw* me never speaking to him.

BEN It's been eleven years, Uncle Willie. Hasn't time changed anything for you?

WILLIE Yes. I hate him eleven years more.

BEN Why?

WILLIE Why? . . . You never met him?

BEN Sure I met him. I was fifteen years old. I met him once at that benefit at Madison Square Garden and once backstage at some television show. He seemed nice enough to me.

WILLIE That's only twice. You had to meet him three times to hate him.

BEN Uncle Willie, could I make a suggestion?

WILLIE He used to give me the finger.

BEN The what?

WILLIE The finger! The finger! He would poke me in the chest with the finger. (*He crosses to* BEN *and demonstrates on him by poking a finger in* BEN's *chest every time he makes a point*) He would say, "Listen, Doctor." (*Pokes finger*) "I'm *telling* you, Doctor." (*Pokes finger*) "You know what I *mean*, Doctor." (*Pokes finger.* BEN *rubs his chest in pain*) Hurts, doesn't it? How'd you like it for forty-three years? I got a black and blue hole in my chest. My wife to her dying day thought it was a tattoo. I haven't worked with him in eleven years, it's just beginning to fade away . . . The man had the sharpest finger in show business.

21

BEN   If you work with him again, I promise you I'll buy you a thick padded undershirt.

WILLIE   You think I never did that? One night I put a steel plate under my shirt. He gave me the finger, he had it in a splint for a month.

BEN   Something else must have happened you're not telling me about. You don't work with a person for forty-three years without some bond of affection remaining.

WILLIE   You wanna hear other things? He used to spit in my face. Onstage *the man would spit in my face!*

BEN   Not on purpose.

WILLIE   (*Turns away*) He tells me "not on purpose" . . . If there was some way I could have saved the spit, I would show it to you.

BEN   You mean he would just stand there and spit in your face?

WILLIE   What do you think, he's stupid? He worked it into the act. He would stand with his nose on top of my nose and purposely only say words that began with a "T." (*As he demonstrates, he spits*) "Tootsie Roll." (*Spit*) "Tinker Toy." (*Spit*) "Typing on the typewriter." (*Spits.* BEN *wipes his face*) Some nights I thought I would drown! I don't know where he got it all from . . . I think he would drink all day and save it up for the night.

BEN   I'll put it in the contract. If he spits at you, he won't get paid.

WILLIE   If he can get another chance to spit at me, he wouldn't *want* to get paid.

22

BEN   Then will you answer me one question? If it was all that bad, why did you stick together for forty-three years?

WILLIE   *(Turns; looks at him)* Because he was terrific. There'll never be another one like him . . . Nobody could time a joke the way he could time a joke. Nobody could say a line the way he said it. I knew what he was thinking, he knew what I was thinking. One person, that's what we were . . . No, no. Al Lewis was the best. The *best!* You understand?

BEN   I understand.

WILLIE   As an actor, no one could touch him. As a human being, no one *wanted* to touch him.

BEN   *(Sighs)*   So what do I tell C.B.S.? No deal because Al Lewis spits?

WILLIE   You know when the last time was we worked together?

BEN   Eleven years ago on *The Ed Sullivan Show.*

WILLIE   Eleven years ago on *The Ed Sullivan Show.* July twenty-seventh. He wouldn't put us on in the winter when people were watching, but never mind. We did The Doctor and the Tax Examination. You never saw that, did you?

BEN   No, but I heard it's wonderful.

WILLIE   What about a "classic"? A *classic!* A *dead* person watching that sketch would laugh. We did it maybe eight thousand times, it never missed . . . *That* night it missed. Something was wrong with him, he was rushing, his timing was off, his mind was someplace else. I

23

thought he was sick. Still, we got terrific applause. Five times Ed Sullivan said, "How about that?" We got back into the dressing room, he took off his make-up, put on his clothes, and said to me, "Willie, if it's all the same to you, I'm retiring." I said, "What do you mean, retiring? It's not even nine o'clock. Let's have something to eat." He said, "I'm not retiring for the night. I'm retiring for what's left of my life." And he puts on his hat, walks out of the theater, becomes a stockbroker and I'm left with an act where I ask questions and there's no one there to answer. Never saw the man again to this day. Oh, he called me, I wouldn't answer. He wrote me, I tore it up. He sent me telegrams, they're probably still under the door.

BEN Well, Uncle Willie, with all due respect, you really weren't getting that much work any more. Maybe he was getting tired of doing the same thing for forty-three years. I mean a man has a right to retire when he wants, doesn't he?

WILLIE Not him. Don't forget, when he retired himself, he retired me too. And goddamn it, I wasn't ready yet. Now suddenly maybe he needs five thousand dollars, and he wants to come crawling back, the hell with him. I'm a single now . . .

BEN I spoke to Al Lewis on the phone last night. He doesn't even care about the money. He just wants to do the show for old times' sake. For his grandchildren who never saw him.

WILLIE Sure. He probably retired broke from the stock market. I guarantee you *those* high-class people never got a spit in the face once.

BEN Did you know his wife died two years ago? He's living with his daughter now, somewhere in New Jersey. He doesn't do anything any more. He's got very bad arthritis, he's got asthma, he's got poor blood circulation—

WILLIE I'll send him a pump. He'll outlive *you*, believe me.

BEN He wants very much to do this show, Willie.

WILLIE With arthritis? Forget it. Instead of a finger, he'll poke me with a cane.

BEN C.B.S. wants you to do the doctor sketch. Lewis told me he could get on a stage tonight and do that sketch letter perfect. He doesn't even have to rehearse it.

WILLIE I don't even want to discuss it . . . And in the second place, I would definitely not do it without a rehearsal.

BEN All right, then will you agree to this? Just rehearse with him one day. If it doesn't work out, we'll call it off.

WILLIE I don't trust him. I think he's been planning this for eleven years. We rehearse all week and then he walks out on me just before the show.

BEN Let me call him on the phone. (*Going over to the phone*) Let me set up a rehearsal time for Monday.

WILLIE WAIT A MINUTE! I got to think about this.

BEN We don't have that much time. C.B.S. is waiting to hear.

WILLIE   What's their rush? What are they, going out of business?

BEN   (*Picks up the phone*)   I'm dialing. I'm dialing him, Uncle Willie, okay?

WILLIE   Sixty-forty—I get six thousand, he gets four thousand . . . What the hell can he buy in New Jersey anyway?

BEN   (*Holding the phone*)   I can't do that, Uncle Willie . . . God, I hope this works out.

WILLIE   Tell him I'm against it. I want him to know. I'll do it with an "against it."

BEN   It's ringing.

WILLIE   And he's got to come here. I'm not going there, you understand?

BEN   He's got to be home. I told him I would call about one.

WILLIE   Sure. You know what he's doing? He practicing spitting.

BEN   (*Into the phone*)   Hello? . . . Mr. Lewis? . . . Ben Silverman . . . Yes, fine, thanks . . . I'm here with him now.

WILLIE   Willie Clark. The one he left on *The Ed Sullivan Show*. Ask him if he remembers.

BEN   It's okay, Mr. Lewis . . . Uncle Willie said yes.

WILLIE   With an "against it." Don't forget the "against it."

BEN   No, he's very anxious to do it.

WILLIE *(Jumping up in anger)*   WHO'S ANXIOUS? I'M AGAINST IT! TELL HIM, you lousy nephew.

BEN   Can you come here for rehearsal on Monday? . . . Oh, that'll be swell . . . In the morning. *(To* WILLIE*)* About eleven o'clock? How long is the drive. About two hours?

WILLIE   Make it nine o'clock.

BEN   Be reasonable, Willie. *(Into the phone)* Eleven o'clock is fine, Mr. Lewis . . . Can you give me your address, please, so I can send you the contracts? *(He takes a pen out of his pocket and writes in his notebook)* One-one-nine, South Pleasant Drive . . .

WILLIE   Tell him if he starts with the spitting or poking, I'm taking him to court. I'll have a man on the show watching. Tell him.

BEN   West Davenport, New Jersey . . . Oh-nine-seven-seven-oh-four . . .

WILLIE   I don't want any—*(Spitting)*—"Toy telephones tapping on tin turtles." Tell him. Tell him.
                              Curtain

It is the following Monday, a few minutes before eleven in the morning.

The stage is empty. Suddenly the bathroom door opens and WILLIE *emerges. He is still wearing his slippers and the same pajamas, but instead of his bathrobe, he has made a concession to the occasion. He is wearing a double-breasted blue suit-jacket, buttoned, and he is putting a handkerchief in his pocket. He looks in the mirror, and brushes back his hair. He shuffles over to the window and looks out.*

There is a knock on the door. WILLIE *turns and stares at it. He doesn't move. There is another knock, and then we hear* BEN's *voice.*

BEN's VOICE Uncle Willie. It's Ben.

WILLIE Ben? Is that you?

BEN's VOICE Yes. Open up. (WILLIE *starts toward the door, then stops*)

WILLIE You're alone or he's with you?

BEN's VOICE I'm alone.

WILLIE *(Nods)* Wait a minute. (*The latch is locked again, and again he has trouble getting it open*) Wait a minute.

BEN'S VOICE   Slide it, don't push it.

WILLIE   Wait a minute. I'll push it.

BEN'S VOICE   *DON'T* PUSH IT! SLIDE IT!

WILLIE   Wait a minute. *(He gets the lock open and opens the door.* BEN *walks in)* You're supposed to slide it.

BEN   I rushed like crazy. I didn't want him getting here before me. Did he call or anything?

WILLIE   Where's the *Variety?*

BEN   *(Taking off his coat)* It's Monday, not Wednesday. Didn't you know it was Monday?

WILLIE   I remembered, but I forgot.

BEN   What are you wearing? What is that? You look half-dressed.

WILLIE   Why, for him I should get *all* dressed?

BEN   Are you all right? Are you nervous or anything?

WILLIE   Why should *I* be nervous? *He* should be nervous. I don't get nervous.

BEN   Good.

WILLIE   Listen, I changed my mind. I'm not doing it.

BEN   *What?*

WILLIE   Don't get so upset. Everything is the same as before, except I'm not doing it.

BEN   When did you decide this?

WILLIE   I decided it when you asked me.

BEN   No, you didn't. You told me you *would* do it.

WILLIE   Well, it was a bad decision. This time I made a good one.

BEN   Well, I'm sorry, you have to do it. I've already told C.B.S. that you would be rehearsing this week and, more important, that man is on his way over here now and I'm not going to tell him that you called it off.

WILLIE   We'll leave him a note outside the door.

BEN   We're not leaving any notes. That's why I came here this morning, I was afraid you would try something like this. I'm going to stay until I think you're both acting like civilized human beings, and then when you're ready to rehearse, I'm going to leave you alone. Is that understood?

WILLIE   I'm sick. I woke up sick today.

BEN   No, you're not.

WILLIE   What are you, a doctor? You're an agent. I'm telling you I'm sick.

BEN   What's wrong?

WILLIE   I think I got hepatitis.

BEN   You don't even know what hepatitis is.

WILLIE   If you got it, what's the difference?

BEN   There's nothing wrong with you except a good case of the nerves. You're not backing out, Willie. I don't care what kind of excuse you make, you're going to go

30

through with this. You promised me you would give it at least one day.

WILLIE I'll pick another day.

BEN TODAY! You're going to meet with him and re-hearse with him TODAY. Now *stop* and just behave yourself.

WILLIE What do you mean, "behave yourself"? Who do you think you're talking to, Susan and Jackie?

BEN *Amanda* and Jackie!—Michael. I wish I were. I can reason with them. And now I'm getting chest pains on Monday.

WILLIE Anyway, he's late. He's purposely coming late to aggravate me.

BEN *(Looking out the window)* He's not late. It's two minutes after eleven.

WILLIE So what is he, early? He's *late!*

BEN You're *looking* to start trouble, I can tell.

WILLIE I was up and dressed at eight o'clock, don't tell me.

BEN Why didn't you shave?

WILLIE Get me the Shick commercial, I'll shave. *(He looks in the mirror)* I really think I got hepatitis. Look how green I look.

BEN You don't get green from hepatitis. You get yellow.

WILLIE Maybe I got a very bad case.

BEN *(Looks at his watch)* Now you got me nervous. I wonder if I should call him? Maybe he's sick.

WILLIE *(Glares at him)* You believe *he's* sick, but me you won't believe . . . Why don't you become *his* nephew?
(Suddenly there is a knock on the door. WILLIE *freezes and stares at it)*

BEN That's him. You want me to get it—

WILLIE Get what? I didn't hear anything.

BEN *(Starts toward the door)* All right, now take it easy. Please just behave yourself and give this a chance. Promise me you'll give it a chance.

WILLIE *(Starts for the kitchen)* I'll give it every possible chance in the world . . . But it's not gonna work.

BEN Where are you going?

WILLIE To make tea. I feel like some hot tea.
(He crosses into the kitchen and closes the curtain. Starts to fill up the kettle with water)

BEN *(Panicky)* NOW? NOW? *(*BEN *looks at him, exasperated; a knock on the door again and* BEN *crosses to it and opens it.* AL LEWIS *stands there. He is also about seventy years old and is dressed in his best blue suit, hat, scarf, and carries a walking stick. He was probably quite a gay blade in his day, but time has slowed him down somewhat. Our first impression is that he is soft-spoken and pleasant—and a little nervous)* Mr. Lewis, how do you do? I'm Ben Silverman.
*(*BEN, *nervous, extends his hand)*

AL How are you? Hello. It's nice to see you. *(His eyes dart around looking for* WILLIE. *He doesn't see him yet)* How do you do? . . . Hello . . . Hello . . . How are you?

BEN We met before, a long time ago. My father took me backstage, I forget the theater. It must have been fifteen, twenty years ago.

AL I remember . . . Certainly . . . It was backstage . . . Maybe fifteen, twenty years ago . . . I forget the theater.

BEN That's right.

AL Sure, I remember.
(*He has walked into the room and shoots a glance toward the kitchen.* WILLIE *doesn't look up from his tea-making*)

BEN Please sit down. Uncle Willie's making some tea.

AL Thank you very much.
(*He sits on the edge of the table*)

BEN (*Trying hard to make conversation*) Er . . . Did you have any trouble getting in from Jersey?

AL My daughter drove me in. She has a car.

BEN Oh. That's nice.

AL A 1972 Chrysler . . . black . . .

BEN Yes, the Chrysler's a wonderful car.

AL The big one . . . the Imperial.

BEN I know. I drove it.

AL My daughter's car?

BEN No, the big Chrysler Imperial. I rented one in California.

AL *(Nods)* No, she owns.

BEN I understand . . . Do you come into New York often?

AL Today's the first time in two years.

BEN Really? Well, how did you find it?

AL My daughter drove.

BEN No, I mean, do you find the city different in the two years since you've been here?

AL It's not my New York.

BEN No, I suppose it's not. *(He shoots a glance toward the kitchen.* WILLIE *still hasn't looked in)* Hey, listen, I'm really very excited about all this. Well, for that matter, everyone in the industry is.

AL *(Nods, noncommittally)* Well, we'll see.
(He looks around the room, scrutinizing it)

BEN *(He calls out toward the kitchen)* Uncle Willie, how we doing? *(No answer. Embarrassed, to* AL*)* I guess it's not boiling yet . . . Oh, listen, I'd like to arrange to have a car pick you up and take you home after you're through rehearsing.

AL My daughter's going to pick me up.

BEN Oh, I see. What time did you say? Four? Five?

AL She's going to call me every hour.

BEN Right . . .
(Suddenly WILLIE *sticks his head out of the kitchen, but looks at* BEN *and not at* AL*)*

34

WILLIE   One tea or two teas?

BEN   Oh, here he is. Well, Uncle Willie, I guess it's been a long time since you two—

WILLIE   One tea or two teas?

BEN   Oh. Er, nothing for me, thanks. I'm just about leaving. Mr. Lewis? Some tea?

AL   *(Doesn't look toward* WILLIE*)*   Tea would be nice, thank you.

BEN *(To* WILLIE*)*   Just the one, Uncle Willie.

WILLIE   You're sure? I got two tea balls. I could dunk again.

BEN *(Looks at his watch)*   No, I've got to get back to the office. Honestly.

WILLIE *(Nods)*   Mm-hmm. One tea.
     (On his way back in, he darts a look at LEWIS, *then goes back into the kitchen. He pulls the curtain shut)*

BEN *(To* LEWIS*)*   Well, er . . . Do you have any questions you want to ask about the show? About the studio or rehearsals or the air date? Is there anything on your mind that I could help you with?

AL   Like what?

BEN   Like, er, the studio? Or the rehearsals? Or air date? Things like that?

AL   You got the props?

BEN   Which props are those?

AL   The props. For the doctor sketch. You gotta have props.

BEN   Oh, props. Certainly. What do you need? I'll tell them.
   (*Takes out a pad; writes*)

AL   You need a desk. A telephone. A pointer. A blackboard. A piece of white chalk, a piece of red chalk. A skeleton, not too tall, a stethoscope, a thermometer, an "ahh" stick—

BEN   What's an "ahh" stick?

AL   To put in your mouth to say "ahh."

BEN   Oh, right, an "ahh" stick.

AL   A look stick, a bottle of pills—

BEN   A look stick? What's a look stick?

AL   A stick to look in the ears. With cotton on the end.

BEN   Right. A look stick.

AL   A bottle of pills. Big ones, like for a horse.

BEN   (*Makes a circle with his two fingers*)   About this big?

AL   That's for a pony. (*Makes a circle using the fingers of both hands*) For a horse is like this. Some bandages, cotton, and eye chart—

BEN   Wait a minute, you're going too fast.

AL   (*Slowly*)   A-desk . . . a-telephone . . . a-pointer . . .

36

BEN   No, I got all that—after the cotton and eye chart.

AL   A man's suit. Size forty. Like the one I'm wearing.

BEN   Also in blue?

AL   What do I need two blue suits— Get me a brown.

BEN   A brown suit. Is that all?

AL   That's all.

WILLIE *(From the kitchen, without looking in)*   A piece of liver.

AL   That's all, plus a piece of liver.

BEN   What kind of liver?

AL   Regular calves' liver. From the butcher.

BEN   Like how much? A pound?

AL   A little laugh is a pound. A big laugh is two pounds. Three pounds with a lot of blood'll bring the house down.

BEN   Is that it?

AL   That's it. And a blonde.

BEN   You mean a woman—

AL   You know a blond nurse that's a man? . . . Big! As big as you can find. With a big chest—a forty-five, a fifty—and a nice bottom.

BEN   You mean a sexy girl with a full, round, rear end?

37

AL *(Spreads hands apart)* About like this. *(Makes a smaller behind with his hands)* This is too small. *(Makes a bigger one)* And this is too big. *(Goes back to the original one)* Like this is perfect.

BEN I know what you mean.

AL If you can bring me pictures, I'll pick out one.

BEN There's a million girls like that around.

AL The one we had was the best. I would call her, but she's maybe fifty-five, sixty.

BEN No, no. I'll get a girl. Anything else?

AL Not for me.

BEN Uncle Willie?

WILLIE *(From the kitchen)* I wasn't listening.

BEN Well, if either of you thinks of anything, just call me. *(Looks at his watch again)* Eleven-fifteen—I've got to go. *(He gets up)* Uncle Willie, I'm going. *(He crosses to* LEWIS *and extends his hand)* Mr. Lewis, I can't express to you enough how happy I am, and speaking for the millions of young people in this country who never had the opportunity of seeing Lewis and Clark work, I just want to say "thank you." To both of you. *(Calls out)* To *both of you*, Uncle Willie.

AL *(Nods)* I hope they won't be disappointed.

BEN Oh, they won't.

AL I know they won't. I'm just saying it.

BEN (*Crosses to the kitchen*) Goodbye, Uncle Willie. I'm going.

WILLIE I'll show you the elevator.

BEN I *know* where it is. I'll call you tonight. I just want to say that this is a very happy moment for me. To see you both together again, reunited . . . The two kings of comedy. (*Big smile*) I'm sure it must be *very exciting* for the both of you, isn't it? (*No answer. They both just stare at him*) Well, it looks like we're off to a great start. I'll call you later . . . Goodbye.
> (*He leaves and closes the door. They are alone. WILLIE carries the two teas to the dining table, where the sugar bowl is. He pours himself a teaspoonful of sugar*)

WILLIE (*Without looking in AL's direction*) Sugar?

AL (*Doesn't turn*) If you got.

WILLIE (*Nods*) I got sugar. (*He bangs the sugar bowl down in front of AL, crosses with his own tea to his leather chair and sits. And then the two drink tea . . . silently and interminably. They blow, they sip, they blow, they sip and they sit. Finally*) You like a cracker?

AL (*Sips*) What kind of cracker?

WILLIE Graham, chocolate, coconut, whatever you want.

AL Maybe just a plain cracker.

WILLIE I don't have plain crackers. I got graham, chocolate and coconut.

AL All right, a graham cracker.

39

WILLIE *(Without turning, points into the kitchen)*
They're in the kitchen, in the closet.
(AL *looks over at him, a little surprised at his un-cordiality. He nods in acknowledgment)*

AL   Maybe later.
(They both sip their tea)

WILLIE *(Long pause)*   I was sorry to hear about Lillian.

AL   Thank you.

WILLIE   She was a nice woman. I always liked Lillian.

AL   Thank you.

WILLIE   And how about you?

AL   Thank God, knock wood—*(Raps knuckles on his cane)*—perfect.

WILLIE   I heard different. I heard your blood didn't circulate.

AL   Not true. My blood circulates . . . I'm not saying *everywhere*, but it circulates.

WILLIE   Is that why you use the cane?

AL   It's not a cane. It's a walking stick . . . Maybe once in a great while it's a cane.

WILLIE   I've been lucky, thank God. I'm in the pink.

AL   I was looking. For a minute I thought you were having a flush.

WILLIE *(Sips his tea)*   You know Sol Burton died?

AL Go on . . . Who's Sol Burton?

WILLIE You don't remember Sol Burton?

AL (*Thinks*) Oh, yes. The manager from the Belasco.

WILLIE That was Sol Bernstein.

AL Not Sol Bernstein. Sol *Burton* was the manager from the Belasco.

WILLIE Sol *Bernstein* was the manager from the Belasco, and it wasn't the Belasco, it was the Morosco.

AL Sid *Weinstein* was the manager from the Morosco. Sol *Burton* was the manager from the Belasco. Sol *Bernstein* I don't know *who* the hell was.

WILLIE How can you remember anything if your blood doesn't circulate?

AL It circulates in my *head*. It doesn't circulate in my *feet*.
    (*He stomps his foot on the floor a few times*)

WILLIE Is anything coming down?

AL Wait a minute. Wasn't Sid Weinstein the songwriter?

WILLIE No for chrissakes! That's SOL BURTON!

AL Who wrote "Lady, lady, be my baby"?

WILLIE That's what I'm telling you! Sol Burton, the lousy songwriter.

AL Oh, *that* Sol Burton . . . He died?

WILLIE Last week.

AL   Where?

WILLIE *(Points)*   In *Variety*.

AL   Sure, now I remember . . . And how is Sol Bernstein?

WILLIE   I didn't read anything.

AL   Good. I always liked Sol Bernstein. *(They quietly sip their tea. AL looks around the room)* So-o-o . . . this is where you live now?

WILLIE   Didn't I always live here?

AL *(Looks again)*   Not in here. You lived in the big suite.

WILLIE   This *is* the big suite . . . Now it's five small suites.
     (AL nods, understanding)

AL *(Looks around)*   That's what they do today. Anything to squeeze a dollar. What do they charge now for a small suite?

WILLIE   The same as they used to charge for the big suite.
     (AL nods, understanding)

AL   I have a very nice room with my daughter in New Jersey. I have my own bathroom. They don't bother me, I don't bother them.

WILLIE   What is it, in the country?

AL   Certainly it's in the country. Where do you think New Jersey is, in the city?

WILLIE *(Shrugs)*   New Jersey is what I see from the bench on Riverside Drive. What have they got, a private house?

AL Certainly it's a private house. It's some big place. Three quarters of an acre. They got their own trees, their own bushes, a nice little swimming pool for the kids they blow up in the summertime, a big swing in the back, a little dog house, a rock garden—

WILLIE A what?

AL A rock garden.

WILLIE What do you mean, a rock garden? You mean for rocks?

AL You never saw a rock garden?

WILLIE And I'm not that anxious.

AL It's beautiful. A Chinaman made it. Someday you'll take a bus and you'll come out and I'll show you.

WILLIE I should drive all the way out to New Jersey on a bus to see a rock garden?

AL You don't even know what I'm talking about. You have to live in the country to appreciate it. I never thought it was possible I could be so happy in the country.

WILLIE You don't mind it's so quiet?

AL (Looks at him) They got noise in New Jersey. But it's a quiet noise. Birds . . . drizzling . . . Not like here with the buses and trucks and screaming and yelling.

WILLIE Well, it's different for you. You like the country better because you're retired. You can sit on a porch, look at a tree, watch a bush growing. You're still not active like me. You got a different temperament, you're a slow person.

AL   I'm a slow person?

WILLIE   You're here fifteen minutes, you still got a whole cup of tea. I'm finished already.

AL   That's right. You're finished, and I'm still enjoying it. That was always the difference with us.

WILLIE   You're wrong. I can get up and make a *second* cup of tea and enjoy it twice as much as you. I like a busy life. That's why I love the city. I gotta be near a phone. I never know when a picture's gonna come up, a musical, a commercial . . .

AL   When did you do a picture?

WILLIE   They're negotiating.

AL   When did you do a musical?

WILLIE   They're talking.

AL   When did you do a commercial?

WILLIE   All the time. I did one last week.

AL   For what?

WILLIE   For, er, for the . . . what's it, the potato chips.

AL   What potato chips?

WILLIE   The big one. The crispy potato chips . . . er . . . you know.

AL   What do I know? I don't eat potato chips.

WILLIE   Well, what's the difference what the name is?

AL They hire you to sell potato chips and you can't remember the name?

WILLIE Did you remember Sol Burton?

AL *(Shrugs)* I'm not selling Sol Burton.

WILLIE Listen, I don't want to argue with you.

AL I didn't come from New Jersey to argue.
(*They sit quietly for a few seconds.* AL *sips his tea;* WILLIE *looks at his empty cup*)

WILLIE *(Finally)* So-o-o . . . What do you think? . . . You want to do the doctor sketch?

AL *(Thinks)* Well, listen, it's very good money. It's only a few days' work, I can be back in New Jersey. If you feel you'd like to do it, then my feeling is I'm agreeable.

WILLIE And my feeling they told you.

AL What?

WILLIE They didn't tell you? My feeling is I'm against it.

AL You're against it?

WILLIE Right. But I'll do it if you want to.

AL I don't want to do it if you're against it. If you're against it, don't do it.

WILLIE What do you care if I'm against it as long as we're doing it? I just want you to know *why* I'm doing it.

AL Don't do me any favors.

45

WILLIE Who's doing you a favor? I'm doing my nephew a favor. It'll be good for him in the business if we do it.

AL You're sure?

WILLIE Certainly I'm sure. It's a big break for a kid like that to get big stars like us.

AL That's different. In that case, I'm against it too but I'll do it.

WILLIE *(Nods)* As long as we understand each other.

AL And I want to be sure you know I'm not doing it for the money. The money goes to my grandchildren.

WILLIE The whole thing?

AL The whole thing. But not now. Only if I die. If I don't die, it'll be for my old age.

WILLIE The same with me.

AL You don't have grandchildren.

WILLIE My *nephew's* children. Sidney and Marvin.

AL *(Nods)* Very good.

WILLIE Okay . . . So-o-o, you wanna rehearse?

AL You're not against rehearsing?

WILLIE Why should I be against rehearsing? I'm only against doing the show. Rehearsing is important.

AL All right, let's rehearse. Why don't we move the furniture, and we'll make the set.
  (They both get up and start to move the furniture

ACT ONE

around. First each one takes a single chair and moves it into a certain position. Then they both take a table and jointly move it away. Then they each take the chair the other one had moved before, and move it into a different place. Every time one moves something somewhere, the other moves it into a different spot. Finally WILLIE *becomes aware that they are getting nowhere)*

WILLIE   Wait a minute, wait a minute. What the hell are we doing here?

AL   I'm fixing up the set, I don't know what you're doing.

WILLIE   You're fixing up the set?

AL   That's right.

WILLIE   You're fixing up the set for the doctor sketch?
(AL *looks at him for a long time without saying a word. It suddenly becomes clear to him)*

AL   Oh, the *doctor* sketch?
(*He then starts to pick up a chair and move it into another position.* WILLIE *does the same with another chair. They both move the table . . . and then they repeat what they did before. Every time one moves a chair, the other one moves the same chair to a different position.* WILLIE *stops and looks again)*

WILLIE   Wait a minute! Wait a minute! We're doing the same goddamn thing. Are you fixing up for the doctor sketch or are you redecorating my apartment?

AL   I'm fixing up for the doctor sketch. If you'd leave what I'm doing alone, we'd be finished.

WILLIE   We'd be finished, but we'd be wrong.

47

AL   Not for the doctor sketch. I know what I'm doing. I did this sketch for forty-three years.

WILLIE   And where was I all that time, taking a smoke? Who did you think did it with you for forty-three years? That was *me*, mister.

AL   Don't call me mister, you know my name. I never liked it when you called me mister.

WILLIE   It's not a dirty word.

AL   It is when you say it.

WILLIE   Forgive me, *sir*.

AL   Let's please, for Pete's sakes, fix up for the doctor sketch.

WILLIE   You think *you* know how to do it? You fix it up.

AL   It'll be my pleasure. (WILLIE *stands aside and watches with arms folded as* AL *proceeds to move table and chairs and stools until he arranges them exactly the way he wants them. Then he stands back and folds his arms the same way*) There! *That's* the doctor sketch!

WILLIE *(Smiles arrogantly)*   For how much money?

AL   I don't want to bet you.

WILLIE   You're afraid to lose?

AL   I'm afraid to *win*. You don't even have enough to buy a box of plain crackers.

WILLIE   —Don't be so afraid you're gonna win—because you're gonna lose! That's not the doctor sketch. That's the gypsy chiropractor sketch.

AL You're positive?

WILLIE I'm *more* than positive. I'm *sure*.

AL All right. Show me the doctor sketch.

WILLIE (*Looks at him confidently, then goes to a chair, picks it up and moves it to the left about four inches, if that much. Then he folds his arms over his chest*) There, *that's* the doctor sketch!

AL (*Looks at him*) You know what you are, Willie? You're a lapalooza.

WILLIE (*Nods*) If I'm a lapalooza, you're a mister.

AL Let's please rehearse the sketch.

WILLIE All right, go outside. I'm in the office.

AL You gonna do the part with the nurse first?

WILLIE You see a nurse here? How can I rehearse with a nurse that's not here?

AL I'm just asking a question. I'm not allowed to ask questions?

WILLIE Ask whatever you want. But try to make them intelligent questions.

AL I beg your pardon. I usually ask the kind of question to the kind of person I'm talking to . . . You get my drift?

WILLIE I get it, mister.

AL All right. Let's skip over the nurse. We'll start from where I come in.

WILLIE   All right, from where you come in. First go out.

AL (*Takes a few steps toward the door, stops and turns*) All right, I'm outside. (*Pantomimes with his fist, knocking on a door*) Knock, knock, knock! I was looking for the doctor.

WILLIE   Wait a minute. You're not outside.

AL   Certainly I'm outside.

WILLIE   If you were outside, you couldn't see me, could you?

AL   No.

WILLIE   Can you see me?

AL   Yes.

WILLIE   So you're not outside. Go *all* the way outside. What the hell kind of a rehearsal is this?

AL   It's a rehearsing rehearsal. Can't you make believe I'm all the way out in the hall?

WILLIE   I could also make believe you were still in New Jersey, but you're not. You're here. Let's have a professional rehearsal, for chrissakes. We ain't got a nurse, but we got a door. Let's use what we got.

AL (*Sighs deeply*) Listen, we're not gonna stop for every little thing, are we? I don't know how many years I got left, I don't wanna spend it rehearsing.

WILLIE   We're not gonna stop for the little things. We're gonna stop for the big things . . . The door is a big thing.

50

AL   All right, I'll go through the door, I'll come in, and then we'll run through the sketch once or twice, and that'll be it for today. All right?

WILLIE   Right . . . Unless another big thing comes up.

AL   *(Glares at him)*   All right, I'm going out. I'll be right back in. *(He crosses to the door, opens it, stops and turns)* If I'm outside and my daughter calls, tell her to pick me up in an hour.
    (He goes out and closes the door behind him)

WILLIE   *(Mumbles, half to himself)*   She can pick you up *now* for all I care. *(He puts his hands behind his back, clasps them, and paces back and forth. He calls out)* All right! Knock, knock, knock!

AL   *(From outside)*   Knock, knock, knock!

WILLIE   *(Screams)*   *Don't say it,* for God's sakes, *do it!* *(To himself)* He probably went *crazy* in the country.

AL   *(From outside)*   You ready?

WILLIE   *(Yells)*   I'm ready. Knock, knock, knock! *(AL knocks three times on the door)* Come in. *(We see and hear the doorknob jiggle, but it doesn't open. This is repeated)* All right, come in already.

AL   *(From outside)*   It doesn't open—it's stuck.

WILLIE   *(Wearily)*   All right, wait a minute. *(He shuffles over to the door and puts his hand on the knob and pulls. It doesn't open)* Wait a minute.
    (He tries again, to no avail)

AL   *(From outside)*   What's the matter?

WILLIE   Wait a minute.
  (*He pulls harder, to no avail*)

AL   Is it locked?

WILLIE   It's not locked. Wait a minute. (*He tries again;
it doesn't open*) It's locked. You better get somebody.
Call the boy downstairs. Sandy. Tell him it's locked.

AL (*From outside*)   Let me try it again.

WILLIE   What are you wasting time? Call the boy. Tell
him it's locked.
  (AL *tries it again, turning it in the other direction,
and the door opens. They stand there face-to-
face*)

AL   I fixed it.

WILLIE (*Glares at him*)   You didn't fix it. You just don't
know how to open a door.

AL   Did my daughter call?

WILLIE   You know, I think you went crazy in the country.

AL   You want to stand here and insult me, or do you want
to rehearse the sketch?

WILLIE   I would like to do *both*, but we ain't got the time
. . . Let's forget the door. Stand in here and say "Knock,
knock, knock."

AL (AL *comes in and closes the door. Sarcastically*)   I hope
I can get *out* again.

WILLIE   I hope so too. (*He places his hands behind his
back and paces*) All right. "Knock, knock, knock."

AL (*Pantomimes with his fist*) Knock, knock, knock.

WILLIE (*Singsong*) Enter!

AL (*Stops and looks at him*) What do you mean "Enter"? (*He does it in the same singsong way*) What happened to "Come in"?

WILLIE It's the same thing, isn't it? "Enter" or "come in." What's the difference, as long as you're in?

AL The difference is we've done this sketch twelve thousand times, and you've always said "Come in," and suddenly today it's "Enter." Why today, after all these years, do you suddenly change it to "Enter"?

WILLIE (*Shrugs*) I'm trying to freshen up the act.

AL Who asked you to freshen up the act? They asked for the doctor sketch, didn't they? The doctor sketch starts with "Come in," not "Enter." You wanna freshen up something, put some flowers in here.

WILLIE It's a new generation today. This is not 1934, you know.

AL No kidding? I didn't get today's paper.

WILLIE What's bad about "Enter" instead of "Come in"?

AL Because it's different. You know why we've been doing it the same way for forty-three years? Because it's good.

WILLIE And you know why we don't do it any more? Because we've been doing it the same way for forty-three years.

AL So, if we're not doing it any more, why are we changing it?

WILLIE Can I make a comment, nothing personal? I think you've been sitting on a New Jersey porch too long.

AL What does that mean?

WILLIE That means I think you've been sitting on a New Jersey porch too long. From my window, I see everything that goes on in the world. I see old people, I see young people, nice people, bad people, I see holdups, drug addicts, ambulances, car crashes, jumpers from buildings—I see everything. You see a lawn mower and a milkman.

AL (*Looks at him for a long moment*) And that's why you want to say "Enter" instead of "Come in"?

WILLIE Are you listening to me?

AL (*Looks around*) Why, there's someone else in the room?

WILLIE You don't know the first thing that's going on today?

AL All right, what's going on today?

WILLIE Did you ever hear the expression "That's where it is"? Well, this is where it is, and that's where I am.

AL I see . . . Did you ever hear the expression "You don't know what the hell you're talking about"? It comes right in front of the *other* expression "You *never* knew what the hell you were talking about."

54

WILLIE *I* wasn't the one who retired. You know why you retired? Because you were tired. You were getting old-fashioned. I was still new-fashioned, and I'll *always* be.

AL I see. That's why you're in such demand. That's why you're such a "hot" property today. That's why you do movies you don't do, that's why you're in musicals you're not in, and that's why you make commercials you don't make—because you can't even remember them to *make* them.

WILLIE You know what I *do* remember? I remember what a pain in the ass you are to work with, that's what I remember.

AL That's right. And when you worked with this pain in the ass, you lived in a *five*-room suite. Now you live in a *one*-room suite . . . And you're still wearing the same goddamn pajamas you wore in the five-room suite.

WILLIE I don't have to take this crap from you.

AL You're lucky you're getting it. No one else wants to give it to you.

WILLIE I don't want to argue with you. After you say "Knock, knock, knock," I'm saying "Enter," and if you don't like it you don't have to come in.

AL You can't say nothing without my permission. I own fifty percent of this act.

WILLIE Then say *your* fifty percent. I'm saying "Enter" in my fifty percent.

AL   If you say "Enter" after "Knock, knock, knock" . . . I'm coming in all right. But not alone. I'm bringing a lawyer with me.

WILLIE   Where? From New Jersey? You're lucky if a *cow* comes with you.

AL   Against *you* in court, I could *win* with a cow.
(*He enunciates each point by poking* WILLIE *in the chest*)

WILLIE (*Slaps his hand away*)   The *finger?* You're start-ing with the finger again?
(*He runs into the kithcen and comes out brandish-ing a knife*)

AL   I'll tell you the truth now. I didn't retire. I *escaped.*

WILLIE (*Wielding the knife*)   The next time you give me the finger, say goodbye to the finger.

AL (*Hiding behind a chair*)   Listen, I got a terrific idea. Instead of working together again, let's never work to-gether again. You're crazy.

WILLIE   I'm crazy, heh? I'M CRAZY!

AL   Keep saying it until you believe it.

WILLIE   I may be crazy, but you're *senile!* You know what that is?

AL   I'm not giving you any straight lines.

WILLIE   Crazy is when you got a couple of parts that go wrong. Senile is when you went the hell out of business. That's you, mister. (*The phone rings.* AL *moves toward the phone*) Get away from that phone. (*He drives the knife into the table.* AL *backs away in shock.* WILLIE *picks up the phone)* Hello?

AL   Is that my daughter?

WILLIE   Hello . . . How are you?

AL   Is that my daughter? Is that her?

WILLIE *(To* AL*)* Will you shut up? Will you be quiet? Can't you see I'm talking? Don't you see me on the phone with a person? For God's sakes, behave like a human being for five seconds, will you? WILL YOU BEHAVE FOR FIVE SECONDS LIKE A HUMAN BEING? *(Into the phone)* Hello? . . . Yes . . . Just a minute. *(To* AL*)* It's your daughter.
     (He sits, opens up Variety*)*

AL *(Takes the phone, turns his back to* WILLIE*, speaks low)* Hello . . . Hello, sweetheart . . . No . . . No . . . I can't talk now . . . I said I can't talk now . . . Because he's a crazy bedbug, that's why.

WILLIE *(Jumps up)* Mister is no good but bedbug is all right?? *(Yells into the phone)* Your father is sick! Come and get your sick father!

AL *(Turns to him)* Don't you see me on the phone with a person? Will you please be quiet, for God's sakes! *(Back into the phone)* Listen, I want you to pick me up now . . . I don't want to discuss it. Pick me up now. In front of the hotel. Don't park too close, it's filthy here . . . I *know* what I promised. Don't argue with me. I'm putting on my coat. I'll wait in the street—I'll probably get mugged . . . All right, just a minute. *(He hands the phone to* WILLIE*)* She'd like to talk to you for a second.

WILLIE Who is it?

AL *(Glares at him)* Mrs. Eleanor Roosevelt . . . What do you mean, who is it? Didn't you just say it's my daughter?

WILLIE I know it's your daughter. I forgot her name.

AL Doris.

WILLIE What does she want?

AL *(Yells)* Am I Doris? She'll tell you.

WILLIE *(Takes the phone)* Hello? . . . Hello, dear, this is Willie Clark . . . Unpleasantness? There was no unpleasantness . . . There was stupidity maybe but no unpleasantness . . .

AL Tell her I'm getting into my coat. *(He is putting his coat on)* Tell her I got one sleeve on.

WILLIE *(Into the phone)* I was hoping it would work out too . . . I bent over backwards and forwards. He didn't even bend sideways . . .

AL I got the other sleeve on . . . Tell her I'm up to my hat and then I'm out the door.

WILLIE It's a question of one word, darling. "Enter"! . . . "Enter"—that's all it comes down to.

AL *(Puts his hat on)* The hat is on. I'm bundled up, tell her.

WILLIE *(Into the phone)* Yes . . . Yes, I will . . . I'll tell him myself. I promise . . . Goodbye, Dorothy. *(He hangs up)* I told her we'll give it one more chance.

AL   Not if you say "Enter." "Come in," I'll stay. "Enter," I go.

WILLIE   Ask me "Knock, knock, knock."

AL   Don't fool around with me. I got enough pains in my
neck. Are you going to say "Come in"?

WILLIE   Ask me "Knock, knock, knock."

AL   I know you, you bastard!

WILLIE   ASK ME "KNOCK, KNOCK, KNOCK"!

AL   KNOCK, KNOCK, KNOCK!

WILLIE (*Grinding it in*)   EN-TERRR!

AL   BEDBUG! CRAZY BEDBUG!
       (*He starts to run out*)

WILLIE (*Big smile*)   ENNN-TERRRRR!
       (*The curtain starts down*)

AL (*Heading for the door*)   LUNATIC BASTARD!

WILLIE   ENNN-TERRRR!
                    Curtain

ACT
TWO

*The scene is a doctor's office or, rather, an obvious
stage "flat" representation of a doctor's office. It has an old
desk and chair, a telephone, a cabinet filled with medicine
bottles, a human skeleton hanging on a stand, a blackboard
with chalk and pointer, an eye chart on the wall.*

*Overhead television lights surround the top of the
set. Two boom microphones extend from either end of the
set over the office.*

*At rise, the set is not fully lit. A thin, frail man in
a hat and business suit sits in the chair next to the doctor's
desk, patiently waiting.*

VOICE OF TV DIRECTOR *(Over the loudspeaker)* Eddie!
EDDIE!
> *(EDDIE, a young assistant TV director with headset
> and speaker, trailing wires and carrying a clipboard,
> steps out on the set. He speaks through his mike)*

EDDIE Yeah, Phil?

VOICE OF TV DIRECTOR Any chance of doing this today?

EDDIE *(Shrugs)* We're all set here, Phil. We're just waiting on the actors.

VOICE OF TV DIRECTOR What the hell is happening?

63

EDDIE   I don't know. There's a problem with the make-up. Mr. Clark wants a Number Seven amber or something.

VOICE OF TV DIRECTOR   Well, get it for him.

EDDIE   Where? They stopped making it thirty-four years ago.

VOICE OF TV DIRECTOR   Christ!

EDDIE   And Mr. Lewis says the "ahh" sticks are too short.

VOICE OF TV DIRECTOR   The what?

EDDIE   The "ahh" sticks. Don't ask me. I'm still trying to figure out what a "look" stick is.

VOICE OF TV DIRECTOR   What the hell are we making, *Nicholas and Alexandra?* Tell them it's just a dress rehearsal. We'll worry about the props later. Let's get moving, Eddie. Christ Almighty.
   (WILLIE's *nephew* BEN *appears onstage. He talks up into the overhead mike*)

BEN   Mr. Schaefer . . . Mr. Schaefer, I'm awfully sorry about the delay. Mr. Lewis and Mr. Clark have had a few technical problems backstage.

VOICE OF TV DIRECTOR   Yeah, well, we've had it all week . . . I'm afraid we're running out of time here. I've got twelve goddamned other numbers to get through today.

BEN   I'll get them right out. There's no problem.

VOICE OF TV DIRECTOR   Tell them I want to run straight through, no stopping. They can clean up whatever they want afterwards.

ACT TWO

BEN Absolutely.

VOICE OF TV DIRECTOR I haven't seen past "Knock, knock, knock"—"Come in" since Tuesday.

BEN *(Looks offstage)* Right. There they are. *(Into the mike)* We're ready, Mr. Schaefer. I'll tell them we're going to go straight through, no stopping. Thank you very much.
  (BEN *exits very quickly*)

VOICE OF TV DIRECTOR All right, Eddie, bring in the curtains.

EDDIE What?

VOICE OF TV DIRECTOR Bring in the curtains. Let's run it from the top with the voice over.

EDDIE *(Calls up)* Let's have the curtains.
  (The curtains come in)

VOICE OF TV DIRECTOR Voice over!

ANNOUNCER The golden age of comedy reached its zenith during a fabulous and glorious era known as Vaudeville —Fanny Brice, W. C. Fields, Eddie Cantor, Ed Wynn, Will Rogers and a host of other greats fill its Hall of Fame. There are two other names that belong on this list, but they can never be listed separately. They are more than a team. They are two comic shining lights that beam as one. For, Lewis without Clark is like laughter without joy. We are privileged to present tonight, in their first public performance in over eleven years, for half a century known as "The Sunshine Boys"—Mr. Al Lewis and Mr. Willie Clark, in their beloved scene, "The Doctor Will See You Now."

(The curtain rises, and the set is fully lit. The frail man in the hat is sitting on the chair as WILLIE, *the doctor, dressed in a floor-length white doctor's jacket, a mirror attached to his head and a stethoscope around his neck is looking into the* PATIENT's *mouth, holding his tongue down with an "ahh" stick)*

WILLIE   Open wider and say "Ahh."

PATIENT   Ahh.

WILLIE   Wider.

PATIENT   *Ahhh!*

WILLIE   *(Moves with his back to the audience)*   A little wider.

PATIENT   Ahhh!

WILLIE   *(Steps away)*   Your throat is all right, but you're gonna have some trouble with your stomach.

PATIENT   How come?

WILLIE   You just swallowed the stick.
          (The PATIENT *feels his stomach)*

PATIENT   Is that bad?

WILLIE   It's terrible. I only got two left.

PATIENT   What about getting the stick out?

WILLIE   What am I, a tree surgeon? . . . All right, for another ten dollars, I'll take it out.

PATIENT   That's robbery.

WILLIE Then forget it. Keep the stick.

PATIENT No, no. I'll pay. Take the stick out.

WILLIE Come back tomorrow. On Thursdays I do wood-work. (*The* PATIENT *gets up and crosses to the door, then exits.* WILLIE *calls out*) Oh, Nurse! Nursey!
  (*The* NURSE *enters. She is a tall, voluptuous and overstacked blonde in a tight dress*)

NURSE Did you want me, Doctor?

WILLIE (*He looks at her, knowingly*) Why do you think I hired you? . . . What's your name again?

NURSE Miss MacKintosh. You know, like the apples.

WILLIE (*Nods*) The name I forgot, the apples I remembered . . . Look in my appointment book, see who's next.

NURSE It's a Mr. Kornheiser.

WILLIE Maybe you're wrong. Look in the book. It's better that way.
  (*She crosses to the desk and bends way over as she looks through the appointment book. Her firm, round rear end faces us and* WILLIE. WILLIE *shakes his head from side to side in wonderful contemplation*)

NURSE (*Still down*) No, I was right.

WILLIE So was I.

NURSE (*Straightens up and turns around*) It's Mr. Kornheiser.

WILLIE Are you sure? Spell it.

67

NURSE (*Turns, bends and gives us the same wonderful view again*) K-o-r-n-h-e-i-s-e-r!
(*She turns and straightens up*)

WILLIE (*Nods*) What's the first name?

NURSE (*Turns, bends*) Walter.

WILLIE Stay down for the middle name.

NURSE (*Remains down*) Benjamin.

WILLIE Don't move and give me the whole thing.

NURSE (*Still rear end up, reading*) Walter Benjamin Korn-heiser.
(*She turns and straightens up*)

WILLIE Oh, boy. From now on I only want to see patients with long names.

NURSE Is there anything else you want?

WILLIE Yeah. Call a carpenter and have him make my desk lower.
(*The* NURSE *walks sexily right up to* WILLIE *and stands with her chest practically on his, breathing and heaving*)

NURSE (*Pouting*) Yes, Doctor.

WILLIE (*Wipes his brow*) Whew, it's hot in here. Did you turn the steam on?

NURSE (*Sexily*) No, Doctor.

WILLIE In that case, take a five-dollar raise. Send in the next patient before *I'm* the next patient.

NURSE   Yes, Doctor. *(She coughs)* Excuse me, I think I have a chest cold.

WILLIE   Looks more like an epidemic to me.

NURSE   Yes, Doctor. *(She wriggles her way to the door)* Is there anything else you can think of?

WILLIE   I can *think* of it, but I'm not so sure I can *do* it.

NURSE   Well, If I *can* help you, Doctor, that's what the nurse is for.
   (She exits and closes the door with an enticing look)

WILLIE   I'm glad I didn't go to law school. *(Then we hear three knocks on the door. "Knock, knock, knock")* Aha. That must be my next patient. *(Calls out)* Come in! *(The door starts to open)*—and *enter!*
   (AL steps in and glares angrily at WILLIE. He is in a business suit, wears a wig, and carries a cheap attaché case)

AL   I'm looking for the doctor.

WILLIE   Are you sick?

AL   Are *you* the doctor?

WILLIE   Yes.

AL   I'm not *that* sick.

WILLIE   What's your name, please?

AL   Kornheiser. Walter Benjamin Kornheiser. You want me to spell it?

WILLIE   Never mind. I got a better speller than you . . . *(Takes a tongue depressor from his pocket)* Sit down and open your mouth, please.

69

AL   There's nothing wrong with my mouth.

WILLIE   Then just sit down.

AL   There's nothing wrong with that either.

WILLIE   Then what are you doing here?

AL   I came to examine you.

WILLIE   I think you got everything backwards.

AL   It's possible. I dressed in a hurry this morning.

WILLIE   You mean you came here for me to examine *you*.

AL   No, I came here for me to examine *you*. I'm a tax collector.

WILLIE   *(Nods)* That's nice. I'm a stamp collector. What do you do for a living?

AL   I find out how much money people make.

WILLIE   Oh, a busybody. Make an appointment with the nurse.

AL   I did. I'm seeing her Friday night . . .

WILLIE   *(Jumps up and down angrily)* Don't fool around with my nurse. DON'T FOOL AROUND WITH MY NURSE! She's a nice girl. She's a *Virginian!*

AL   A what?

WILLIE   A *Virginian.* That's where she's from.

AL   Well, she ain't going *back*, I can tell you that. *(He sits, opens the attaché case)* I got some questions to ask you.

WILLIE   I'm too busy to answer questions. I'm a doctor. If you wanna see me, you gotta be a patient.

AL   But I'm not sick.

WILLIE   Don't worry. We'll find something.

AL   All right, you examine me and I'll examine you . . . (*Takes out a tax form as* WILLIE *wields the tongue depressor*) The first question is, How much money did you make last year?

WILLIE   Last year I made—
     (*He moves his lips mouthing a sum, but it's not audible.*)

AL   I didn't hear that.

WILLIE   Oh. Hard of hearing. I knew we'd find something. Did you ever have any childhood diseases?

AL   Not lately.

WILLIE   Father living or deceased?

AL   Both.

WILLIE   What do you mean, both?

AL   First he was living, now he's deceased.

WILLIE   What did your father die from?

AL   My mother . . . Now it's my turn. Are you married?

WILLIE   I'm looking.

AL   Looking to get married?

WILLIE   No, looking to get out.
     (*He looks in* AL's *ear with a flashlight*)

AL   What are you doing?

WILLIE   I'm examining your lower intestines.

AL   So why do you look in the ear?

WILLIE   If I got a choice of two places to look, I'll take this one.

AL   (*Consulting his form*)   Never mind. Do you own a car?

WILLIE   Certainly I own a car. Why?

AL   If you use it for medical purposes, you can deduct it from your taxes. What kind of car do you own?

WILLIE   An ambulance.

AL   Do you own a house?

WILLIE   Can I deduct it?

AL   Only if you use it for medical purposes. Where do you live?

WILLIE   In Mount Sinai Hospital . . . Open your shirt, I want to listen to your heartbeat.

AL   (*Unbuttons two buttons on his shirt*)   Will this take long?

WILLIE   Not if I hear something. (*He puts his ear to* AL's *chest and listens*) Uh-huh. I hear something . . . You're all right.

AL   Aren't you going to listen with the stethoscope?

WILLIE   Oh, sure. I didn't know you wanted a thorough examination. (*Puts the stethoscope to his ears and listens to* AL*'s chest*) Oh, boy. Ohhh, boyyyy! You know what you got?

AL What?

WILLIE A filthy undershirt.

AL Never mind that. Am I in good health?

WILLIE Not unless you change your undershirt.

AL What is this, a doctor's office or a laundry? I bet you never went to medical school.

WILLIE (*Jumping up and down again*) What are you talkin'? . . . WHAT ARE YOU TALKIN'? . . . I went to Columbia Medical School.

AL Did you pass?

WILLIE Certainly.

AL Well, you should have gone *in!*

WILLIE Never mind . . . I'm gonna examine your eyes now.

AL They're perfect. I got twenty-twenty eyes.

WILLIE That's too much. All you need is one and one. Look at that chart on the wall. Now put your left hand over your left eye and your right hand over your right eye. (AL *does so*) Now tell me what you see.

AL I don't see nothing.

WILLIE Don't panic, I can cure you . . . Take your hands away. (AL *does*) Can you see now?

AL Certainly I can see now.

WILLIE You know, I fixed over two thousand people like that.

AL It's a miracle.

WILLIE Thank you.

AL A miracle you're not in jail . . . What do you charge for a visit?

WILLIE A dollar.

AL A dollar? That's very cheap for an examination.

WILLIE It's not an examination. It's just a visit. "Hello and Goodbye" . . . "Hello and How Are You?" is ten dollars.

AL If you ask me, you're a quack.

WILLIE If I was a duck I would ask you . . . Now roll up your sleeve, I wanna take some blood.

AL I can't do it.

WILLIE Why not?

AL If I see blood, I get sick.

WILLIE Do what I do. Don't look.

AL I'm sorry. I'm not giving blood. I'm anemic.

WILLIE What's anemic?

AL You're a doctor and you don't know what anemic means?

WILLIE That's because I'm a specialist.

AL   What do you specialize in?

WILLIE   Everything but anemic.

AL   Listen, can I continue my examination?

WILLIE   You continue yours, and I'll continue mine. All right, cross your legs. (*He hits* AL's *knee with a small hammer*) Does it hurt if I hit you with the hammer?

AL   Yes.

WILLIE   Good. From now on, try not to get hit with a hammer. (*He throws the hammer over his shoulder. He takes a specimen bottle from the cabinet and returns*) You see this bottle?

AL   Yes.

WILLIE   You know what you're supposed to do with this bottle?

AL   I think so.

WILLIE   You *think* so or you *know* so? If you're not sure, let me know. The girl doesn't come in to clean today.

AL   What do you want me to do?

WILLIE   I want you to go in this bottle.

AL   I haven't got time. I have to go over your books.

WILLIE   *The hell you will!*

AL   If I don't go over your books, the *government* will come in here and go over your books.

WILLIE   Don't they have a place in Washington?

AL   Certainly, but they have to go where the books are.

WILLIE   The whole government?

AL   No, just the Treasury Department.

WILLIE   That's a relief.

AL   I'm glad you're relieved.

WILLIE   I wish *you* were before you came in here.
(*The door opens and the big-chested* NURSE *steps in*)

NURSE   Oh, Doctor. Doctor Klockenmeyer.

WILLIE   Yes.

NURSE   Mrs. Kolodny is on the phone. She wants you to rush right over and deliver her baby.

WILLIE   I'm busy now. Tell her I'll mail it to her in the morning.

NURSE   Yes, Doctor.
(*She exits and closes the door*)

AL   Where did you find a couple of nurses like that?

WILLIE   She was standing on Forty-third and Forty-fourth Street . . . Let me see your tongue, please.

AL   I don't want to.
(WILLIE *squeezes* AL's *throat, and his tongue comes out*)

WILLIE   Open the mouth . . . How long have you had that white coat on your tongue?

76

AL   Since January. In the spring I put on a gray sports jacket.

WILLIE   Now hold your tongue with your fingers and say "shish kabob."

AL   *(Holds his tongue with his fingers)*   Thickabob.

WILLIE   Again.

AL   Thickabob.

WILLIE   I have bad news for you.

AL   What is it?

WILLIE   If you do that in a restaurant, you'll never get shish kabob.

AL   *(Stands with his face close to* WILLIE'S*)*   Never mind that. What about your *taxes?*
        (On the "T," he spits a little)

WILLIE   *(Wipes his face)*   The what?

AL   The *taxes.* It's *time to* pay your *taxes* to the *Treasury.*
        (All the "T's" are quite fluid. WILLIE *wipes his face and glares angrily at* AL*)*

WILLIE   I'm warning you, don't start in with me.

AL   What are you talking about?

WILLIE   You know what I'm talking about. *(Illustrates)* "It's *time to* pay the *taxes.*" You're speaking with spitting again.

AL   I said the right line, didn't I? If it comes out juicy, I can't help that.

WILLIE *(Quite angry)* It doesn't come out juicy unless you squeeze the "T's." I'm warning you, don't squeeze them on me.

(VOICE OF TV DIRECTOR *is heard over the loudspeaker*)

VOICE OF TV DIRECTOR Okay, let's hold it a second. Mr. Clark, I'm having trouble with the dialogue. I don't find those last few lines in the script.

WILLIE *(Shouts up)* It's not in the script, it's in *his mouth.*

AL *(Talking up into the mike)* I said the right line. Look in the script, you'll find it there.

WILLIE *(Shouting)* You'll find the words, you won't find the spit. The spit's his own idea. He's doing it on *purpose!*

AL I don't spit on purpose. I spit on accident. I've *always* spitted on accident. It's not possible to say that line without spitting a little.

WILLIE *(Addressing all his remarks to the unseen director)* I can say it. *(He says the line with great delicacy, especially on the "T's")* "It's time to pay your taxes to the Treasury." *(Back to his normal inflection)* There wasn't a spit in my entire mouth. Why doesn't he say it like *that?*

AL What am I, an Englishman? I'm talking the same as I've talked for forty-three years.

VOICE OF TV DIRECTOR Gentlemen, can we argue this point after the dress rehearsal and go one with the sketch?

WILLIE I'm not going to stand here and get a shower in the face. If you want me to go on, either take out the line or get me an umbrella.

VOICE OF TV DIRECTOR   Can we *please* go on? With all due respect, gentlemen, we have twelve other scenes to rehearse and we cannot spend all day on personal squabbles . . .

WILLIE   I'll go on, but I'm moving to a safer spot.

VOICE OF TV DIRECTOR   Don't worry about the moves, we'll pick you up on camera. Now, let's skip over this spot and pick it up on "I hope you don't have what Mr. Melnick had." (WILLIE *moves away from* AL) All right, Mr. Clark, whenever you're ready.

WILLIE   (*Waits a minute, then goes back into the doctor character*) I hope you don't have what Mr. Melnick had.

AL   What did Mr. Melnick have?

WILLIE   (*Points to standing skeleton*) Ask him yourself, he's standing right there.

AL   That's Mr. Melnick?

WILLIE   It could be *Mrs.* Melnick. Without high heels, I can't tell.

AL   If he's dead, why do you leave him standing in the office?

WILLIE   He's still got one more appointment with me.

AL   (*Crosses to him*) You know what you are? You're a charlatan! (*As* AL *says that line, he punctuates each word by poking* WILLIE *in the chest with his finger. It does not go unnoticed by* WILLIE) Do you know what a charlatan is?
(*More pokes*)

79

WILLIE   It's a city in North Carolina. And if you're gonna poke me again like that, you're gonna end up in Poughkeepsie.

VOICE OF TV DIRECTOR *(Over the loudspeaker)* Hold it, hold it. Where does it say, "You're going to end up in Poughkeepsie"?

WILLIE *(Furious)* Where does it say he can poke me in the chest? He's doing it on purpose. He *always* did it on purpose, just to get my goat.

AL *(Looking up to the mike)* I didn't poke him, I tapped him. A light little tap, it wouldn't hurt a baby.

WILLIE   Maybe a baby elephant. I *knew* I was going to get poked. First comes the spitting, then comes the poking. I know his routine already.

AL *(To the mike)* Excuse me. I'm sorry we're holding up the rehearsal, but we have a serious problem on our hands. The man I'm working with is a lunatic.

WILLIE *(Almost in a rage)* *I'm* a lunatic, heh? He breaks my chest and spits in my face and calls *me* a lunatic! I'm gonna tell you something now I never told you in my entire life. I hate your guts.

AL   You told it to me on Monday.

WILLIE   Then I'm telling it to you again.

VOICE OF TV DIRECTOR   Listen, gentlemen, I really don't see any point in going on with this rehearsal.

AL   I don't see any point in going on with this *show*. This man is persecuting me. For eleven years he's been waiting to get back at me, only I'm not gonna give him the chance.

(*The assistant director,* EDDIE, *walks out in an attempt to make peace*)

WILLIE (*Half-hysterical*) I knew it! I knew it! He planned it! He's been setting me up for eleven years just to walk out on me again.

EDDIE (*Trying to be gentle*) All right, Mr. Clark, let's settle down. Why don't we all go into the dressing room and talk this out?

AL I didn't want to do it in the first place.

WILLIE (*Apoplectic*) Liar! Liar! His daughter *begged* me on the phone. She *begged* me!

(BEN *rushes out to restrain* WILLIE)

BEN Uncle Willie, please, that's enough. Come back to the dressing room.

EDDIE Gentlemen, we need the stage. Can we please do this over on the side?

AL (*To the assistant director*) The man is hysterical, you can see for yourself. He's been doing this to me all week long.

(*He starts taking off the wig and suit jacket*)

WILLIE Begged me. She begged me. His own daughter begged me.

BEN Uncle Willie, stop, please.

AL (*To the others*) I'm sorry we caused everyone so much trouble. I should have stayed in New Jersey in the first place. (*On his way out. To the assistant director*)

He pulled a knife on me last week. In his own apartment he pulled a knife on me. A crazy man.
(He is gone)

WILLIE   I don't need you. I *never* needed you. You were nothing when I found you, and that's what you are today.

BEN   Come on, Willie. *(Out front)* I'm sorry about this, Mr. Schaefer.

WILLIE   He thinks I can't get work without him. Maybe *his* career is over, but not mine. Maybe he's finished, but not me. You hear? not me! NOT M—
(He clutches his chest)

BEN   *(Turns and sees him stagger)*   Grab him, quick! (EDDIE *rushes to* WILLIE, *but it's too late—*WILLIE *falls to the floor.* BEN *rushes to his side)* All right, take it easy, Uncle Willie, just lie there. *(To* EDDIE*)* Get a doctor, please hurry.
(A bit actor and the NURSE *rush onstage behind* BEN*)*

WILLIE   *(Breathing hard)*   I don't need a doctor. Don't get a doctor, I don't trust them.

BEN   Don't talk, Willie, you're all right. *(To the* NURSE*)* Somebody get a blanket, please.

WILLIE   *(Breathing fast)*   Don't tell him. Don't tell him I fell down. I don't want to give him the satisfaction.

BEN   Of course, I won't tell him, Willie. There's nothing to tell. You're going to be all right.

WILLIE   Frito-Lays . . . That's the name of the potato chip . . . You see? I remembered . . . I remembered the name! Frito-Lays.

(BEN *is holding* WILLIE's *hand as the lights dim. The curtain falls on the scene. In the dark, we hear the voice of the* ANNOUNCER)

ANNOUNCER   The golden age of comedy reached its zenith during a fabulous and glorious era known as Vaudeville —Fanny Brice, W. C. Fields, Eddie Cantor, Ed Wynn, Will Rogers and a host of other greats fill its Hall of Fame. There are two other names that belong on this list, but they can never be listed separately. They are more than a team. They are two comic shining lights that beam as one. For, Lewis without Clark is like laughter without joy. When these two greats retired, a comic style disappeared from the American scene that will never see its likes again . . . Here, then, in a sketch taped nearly eleven years ago on *The Ed Sullivan Show*, are Lewis and Clark in their classic scene, "The Doctor Will See You Now."

(*We hear* WILLIE's *voice and that of the first* PATIENT)

WILLIE   Open wider and say "Ahh."

PATIENT   Ahh.

WILLIE   Wider.

PATIENT   Ahh.

WILLIE   A little wider.

PATIENT   Ahhh!

WILLIE   Your throat is all right, but you're gonna have some trouble with your stomach.

PATIENT   How come?

WILLIE   You just swallowed the stick.

SCENE 2

The curtain rises. The scene is WILLIE'S *hotel room, two weeks later. It is late afternoon.* WILLIE *is in his favorite pajamas in bed, propped up on the pillows, his head hanging down, asleep.*

The television is droning away—another daytime serial. A black REGISTERED NURSE *in uniform, a sweater draped over her shoulders, and her glasses on a chain around her neck, is sitting in a chair watching the television. She is eating from a big box of chocolates. Two very large vases of flowers are on the bureau.* WILLIE'S *head bobs a few times; then he opens his eyes.*

WILLIE   What time is it?

NURSE *(Turns off the TV and glances at her watch)*   Ten to one.

WILLIE   Ten to one? . . . Who are you?

NURSE   Don't give me that. You know who I am.

WILLIE   You're the same nurse from yesterday?

NURSE   I'm the same nurse from every day for two weeks now. Don't play your games with me.

WILLIE   I can't even chew a piece of bread, who's gonna play games? . . . Why'd you turn off the television?

84

NURSE It's either watching that or watching you sleep—
either one ain't too interesting.

WILLIE I'm sorry. I'll try to sleep more entertaining . . .
What's today, Tuesday?

NURSE Wednesday.
        (*She bites into a piece of chocolate*)

WILLIE How could this be Wednesday? I went to sleep
on Monday.

NURSE Haven't we already seen Mike Douglas twice this
week?

WILLIE Once.

NURSE Twice.

WILLIE (*Reluctantly*) All right, twice . . . I don't even
remember. I was all right yesterday?

NURSE We are doing very well.

WILLIE We are? When did *you* get sick?

NURSE (*Deadly serious, no smile*) That's funny. That is
really funny, Mr. Clark. Soon as I get home tonight I'm
gonna bust out laughing.

WILLIE You keep eating my candy like that, you're gonna
bust out a lot sooner.

NURSE Well, *you* can't eat it and there's no sense throwing
it out. I'm just storing up energy for the winter.

WILLIE Maybe you'll find time in between the nougat and
the peppermint to take my pulse.

NURSE   I took it. It's a little better today.

WILLIE   When did you take my pulse?

NURSE   When you were sleeping.

WILLIE   *Everybody's* pulse is good when they're sleeping. You take a pulse when a person is up. Thirty dollars a day, she takes a sleeping pulse. I'll tell you the truth, I don't think you know what you're doing . . . and I'm not a prejudiced person.

NURSE   Well, *I* am: I don't like sick people who tell registered nurses how to do their job. You want your tea now?

WILLIE   I don't want to interrupt your candy.

NURSE   And don't get fresh with me. You can get fresh with your nephew, but you can't get fresh with me. Maybe *he* has to take it, but I'm not a blood relative.

WILLIE   That's for sure.

NURSE   That's even funnier than the other one. My *whole* evening's gonna be taken up tonight with nothing but laughing.

WILLIE   I don't even eat candy. Finish the whole box. When you're through, I hope you eat the flowers too.

NURSE   You know why I don't get angry at anything you say to me?

WILLIE   I give up. Why?

NURSE   Because I have a good sense of humor. I am *known* for my good sense of humor. That's why I can take anything you say to me.

WILLIE If you nurse as good as your sense of humor, I won't make it to Thursday . . . Who called?

NURSE No one.

WILLIE I thought I heard the phone.

NURSE *(Gets up)* No one called. *(She crosses and puffs up his pillow)* Did you have a nice nap?

WILLIE It was a nap, nothing special . . . Don't puff up the pillows, please. *(He swats her hands away)* It takes me a day and a night to get them the way I like them, and then you puff them up.

NURSE Oh, woke up a little grouchy, didn't we?

WILLIE Stop making yourself a partner all the time. I woke up grouchy. Don't make the bed, please. I'm still sleeping in it. Don't make a bed with a person in it.

NURSE Can't stand to have people do things for you, can you? If you just want someone to sit here and watch you, you're better off getting a dog, Mr. Clark. I'll suggest that to your nephew.

WILLIE Am I complaining? I'm only asking for two things. Don't take my pulse when I'm sleeping and don't make my bed when I'm in it. Do it the other way around and then we're in business.

NURSE It doesn't bother me to do nothing as long as I'm getting paid for it.
      (She sits)

WILLIE *(A pause)* I'm hungry.

NURSE You want your junket?

WILLIE   Forget it. I'm not hungry. *(She reads)* Tell me something, how old is a woman like you?

NURSE   That is none of your business.

WILLIE   I'm not asking for business.

NURSE   I am fifty-four years young.

WILLIE   Is that so? . . . You're married?

NURSE   My husband passed away four years ago.

WILLIE   Oh . . . You were the nurse?

NURSE   No, I was not the nurse . . . You could use some sleep and I could use some quiet.
        (She gets up)

WILLIE   You know something? For a fifty-four-year-old registered widow, you're an attractive woman.
        (He tries to pat her. She swings at him)

NURSE   And don't try that with me!

WILLIE   Who's trying anything?

NURSE   You are. You're getting fresh in a way I don't like.

WILLIE   What are you worried about? I can't even put on my slippers by myself.

NURSE   I'm not worried about your slippers. And don't play on my sympathy. I don't have any, and I ain't expecting any coming in, in the near future.

WILLIE   Listen, how about a nice alcohol rub?

NURSE   I just gave you one.

WILLIE   No, I'll give *you* one.

NURSE   I know you just say things like that to agitate me.
You like to agitate people, don't you? Well, I am not an
agitatable person.

WILLIE   You're right. I think I'd be better off with the
dog.

NURSE   How did your poor wife stand a man like you?

WILLIE   Who told you about my poor wife?

NURSE   Your poor nephew . . . Did you ever think of getting married again?
(She takes his pulse)

WILLIE   What is this, a proposal?

NURSE   *(Laughs)* Not from me . . . I am *not* thinking of
getting married again . . . Besides, you're just not my
type.

WILLIE   Why? It's a question of religion?

NURSE   It's a question of age. You'd wear me out in no
time.

WILLIE   You think I can't support you? I've got Medicare.

NURSE   You never stop, do you?

WILLIE   When I stop, I won't be here.

NURSE   Well, that's where you're gonna be unless you
learn to slow up a little.

WILLIE Slow up? I moved two inches in three weeks, she tells me slow up.

NURSE I mean, if you're considering getting well again, you have to stop worrying about telephone calls and messages, and especially about when you're going back to work.

WILLIE I'm an actor—I have to act. It's my profession.

NURSE Your profession right now is being a sick person. And if you're gonna act anywhere, it's gonna be from a sick bed.

WILLIE Maybe I can get a job on Marcus Welby.

NURSE You can turn everything I say into a vaudeville routine if you want, but I'm gonna give you a piece of advice, Mr. Clark . . .

WILLIE What?

NURSE The world is full of sick people. And there just ain't enough doctors or nurses to go around to take care of all these sick people. And all the doctors and all the nurses can do just so much, Mr. Clark. But God, in His Infinite Wisdom, has said He will help those who help themselves.

WLLIE (*Looks at her*) So? What's the advice?

NURSE *Stop bugging me!*

WILLIE All right, I'll stop bugging you . . . I don't even know what the hell it means.

NURSE That's better. Now you're my type again.
(*The doorbell rings. The* NURSE *crosses to the door*)

WILLIE   Here comes today's candy.
(*She opens the door.* BEN *enters with packages*)

BEN   Hello. How is he?

NURSE   Fine. I think we're gonna get married.

BEN   Hey, Uncle Willie, you look terrific.

WILLIE   You got my *Variety?*

BEN   (*Goes over to him, and hands him* Variety)   I also got about two hundred get-well telegrams from just about every star in show business—Lucille Ball, Milton Berle, Bob Hope, the mayor. It'll take you nine months just to answer them.

WILLIE   What about a commercial? Did you hear from Alka-Seltzer?

BEN   We have plenty of time to talk about that . . . Miss O'Neill, did you have your lunch yet?

NURSE   Not yet.

WILLIE   She just finished two pounds of appetizers.

BEN   Why don't you go out, take an hour or so? I'll be here for a while.

NURSE   Thank you. I could use some fresh air. (*Gets her coat. To* WILLIE) Now, when I'm gone, I don't want you getting all agitated again, you hear?

WILLIE   I hear, I hear. Stop bugging me.

NURSE   And don't get up to go to the bathroom. Use the you-know-what.

WILLIE (*Without looking up from his* Variety) And if not, I'll do it you-know-where.
(*The* NURSE *exits*)

BEN (*Pulling up a chair next to the bed*) Never mind, she's a very good nurse.

WILLIE (*Looks in the paper*) Oh, boy, Bernie Eisenstein died.

BEN Who?

WILLIE Bernie Eisenstein. Remember the dance team "Ramona and Rodriguez"? Bernie Eisenstein was Rodriguez . . . He would have been seventy-eight in August.

BEN (*Sighs*) Uncle Willie, could you put down *Variety* for a second?

WILLIE (*Still reading*) Did you bring a cigar?

BEN Uncle Willie, you realize you've had a heart attack, don't you? . . . You've been getting away with it for years—the cigars, the corned beef sandwiches, the tension, the temper tantrums. You can't do it any more, Willie. Your heart's just not going to take it.

WILLIE This is the good news you rushed up with? For this we could have skipped a Wednesday.

BEN (*A pause*) I talked to the doctor this morning . . . and I'm going to have to be very frank and honest with you, Willie . . . You've got to retire. I mean give it up. Show business is out.

WILLIE Until when?

BEN Until *ever!* Your blood pressure is abnormally high, your heart is weak—if you tried to work again you would kill yourself.

WILLIE All right, let me think it over.

BEN *Think what over?* There's nothing to think over. You can't work any more, there's no decision to be made. Can't you understand that?

WILLIE You decide for Ben Silverman, I'll decide for Willie Clark.

BEN No, *I'll* decide for Willie Clark. I am your closest and *only* living relative, and I am responsible for your welfare . . . You can't live here any more, Willie. Not alone . . . And I can't afford to keep this nurse on permanently. Right now she's making more than I am. Anyway she already gave me her notice. She's leaving Monday. She's going to Buffalo to work for a very wealthy family.

WILLIE Maybe she'll take me. I always did well in Buffalo.

BEN Come on, Willie, face the facts. We have to do something, and we have to do it quickly.

WILLIE I can't think about it today. I'm tired, I'm going to take a nap.
    (*He closes his eyes and drops his head to the side on the pillow*)

BEN You want to hear my suggestion?

WILLIE I'm napping. Don't you see my eyes closed?

BEN I'd like you to move in with me and Helen and the kids. We have the small spare room in the back, I think

93

you would be very comfortable . . . Uncle Willie, did you hear what I said?

WILLIE   What's the second suggestion?

BEN   What's the matter with the first?

WILLIE   It's not as good as the second.

BEN   I haven't made any yet.

WILLIE   It's still better than the first. Forget it.

BEN   Why?

WILLIE   I don't like your kids. They're noisy. The little one hit me in the head with a baseball bat.

BEN   And I've also seen you talk to them for hours on end about vaudeville and had the time of your life. Right?

WILLIE   If I stopped talking, they would hit me with the bat. No offense, but I'm not living with your children. If you get rid of them, then we'll talk . . .

BEN   I know the reason you won't come. Because Al Lewis lives with his family, and you're just trying to prove some stupid point about being independent.

WILLIE   What's the second suggestion?

BEN   *(A long sigh)*   All right . . . Now, don't jump when I say this, because it's not as bad as it sounds.

WILLIE   Say it.

BEN   There's the Actors' Home in New Brunswick—

WILLIE It's as bad as it sounds.

BEN You're wrong. I drove out there last Sunday and they showed me around the whole place. I couldn't believe how beautiful it was.

WILLIE You went out there? You didn't have the decency to wait until I turned down living with you first?

BEN I just went out to investigate, that's all. No commitments.

WILLIE The Old Actors' Home: the first booking you got me in ten years.

BEN It's on a lake, it's got twenty-five acres of beautiful grounds, it's an old converted mansion with a big porch . . .

WILLIE I knew it. You got me on a porch in New Jersey. He put you up to this, didn't he?

BEN You don't have to sit on the porch. There's a million activities there. They put on shows every Friday and Saturday night. I mean, it's all old actors—what could be better for you?

WILLIE Why New Jersey? I hate New Jersey . . . I'm sorry they ever finished the George Washington Bridge.

BEN I couldn't get over how many old actors were there that I knew and remembered. I thought they were all dead.

WILLIE Some recommendation. A house in the swamps with forgotten people.

BEN They're not forgotten. They're well taken care of . . . Uncle Willie, I promise you, if you spend one day there that you're not happy, you can come back and move in with me.

WILLIE That's my choice—New Jersey or the baseball bat.

BEN All right, I feel a lot better about everything.

WILLIE And what about you?

BEN What do you mean what about me?

WILLIE (*A pause; looks away*) I won't see you no more?

BEN Certainly you'll see me. As often as I can . . . Did you think I wouldn't come to visit you, Uncle Willie?

WILLIE Well, you know . . . People don't go out to New Jersey unless they have to.

BEN Uncle Willie, I'll be there every week. *With* the *Variety*. I'll even bring Helen and the kids.

WILLIE *Don't bring the kids!* Why do you think I'm going to the home for?

BEN You know, this is the first moment since I've known you, that you've treated me like a nephew and not an agent. It's like a whole new relationship.

WILLIE I hope this one works out better than the other one.

BEN I've been waiting for this for fifteen years. You just wouldn't ever let me get close, Uncle Willie.

WILLIE   If you kiss me, I call off the whole thing.

BEN   No kiss, I promise . . . Now there's just one other thing I'd like you to do for me.

WILLIE   With my luck it's a benefit.

BEN   In a way it is a benefit. But not for any organization. It's for another human being.

WILLIE   What are you talking about?

BEN   Al Lewis wants to come and see you.

WILLIE   If you wanted to kill me, why didn't you bring the cigars?

BEN   He's been heartsick ever since this happened.

WILLIE   What do you think I've been? What is this, the mumps?

BEN   You know what I mean . . . He calls me twice a day to see how you are. He's worried to death.

WILLIE   Tonight tell him I'm worse.

BEN   He's not well himself, Willie. He's got diabetes, hardening of the arteries, his eyes are getting very bad . . .

WILLIE   He sees good enough to spit in my face.

BEN   He's lost seven pounds since you were in the hospital. Who do you think's been sending all the candy and flowers every day? He keeps signing other people's names because he knows otherwise you'd throw them out.

WILLIE They're *his* flowers? Throw 'em out!

BEN Uncle Willie, I've never asked you to do a personal favor for me as long as I've known you. But this is important—for me, and for you, for Al Lewis. He won't even stay. He just wants to come up and say hello . . .

WILLIE Hello, heh?

BEN That's all.

WILLIE And if he pokes me in the chest with the finger, I'm a dead man. That's murder, you know.

BEN Come on, Willie. Give us all a break.

WILLIE Well, if he wants to come up, I won't stop him. But I can't promise a "hello." I may be taking a nap.

BEN (*Starts toward the phone*) I knew I could count on you, Willie. He's going to be very happy.
   (*He picks up the phone*)

WILLIE You don't have to call him from here. Why should I pay sixty cents for him to come say hello?

BEN (*He dials "O"*) It's not going to cost you sixty cents. (*To the operator*) Hello. Would you tell the boy at the desk to send Mr. Lewis up to Mr. Clark's room, please? Thank you.
   (*He hangs up*)

WILLIE (*As near to shouting as he can get*) You mean he's here now in the hotel?

BEN He's been with me all morning. I knew it would be all right.

WILLIE First you commit me to the Old Man's Home, bring that bastard here and *then* you ask me?

BEN *(All smiles)* I'm sorry. I apologize. Never speak to me again . . . But just promise you'll be decent to Al Lewis.

WILLIE I'll be wonderful to him. In my will, I'll leave him *you!*
(*He starts to get out of bed*)

BEN What are you doing? You're not supposed to be out of bed.

WILLIE You think I'm going to give him the satisfaction of seeing me laying in bed like a sick person? I'm gonna sit in my chair and I'm gonna look healthier than he does.
(*He tries weakly to get on his slippers*)

BEN The doctor said you're not to get out of bed for *anything.*

WILLIE Lewis coming to apologize to Clark is not anything. To me, this is worth another heart attack. Get my coat from the closet.

BEN *(Starting for the closet)* All right, but just walk slowly, will you, please?
(*He opens the closet*)

WILLIE And then I want you to move my chair all the way back. I want that son-of-a-bitch to have a long walk.

BEN *(Takes out a bathrobe from the closet)* Here, put this on.

WILLIE Not the bathrobe, the jacket. The blue sports jacket. This is gonna be a *formal* apology.

BEN (*Puts back the bathrobe and takes out the blue sports jacket*) He's not coming to apologize. He's just coming to say hello.

WILLIE If he doesn't apologize, I'll drop dead in the chair for spite. And you can tell him that.
(BEN *helps him into the blue sports jacket over the pajamas*)

BEN Now I'm sorry I started in with this.

WILLIE That's funny. Because now I'm starting to feel good. (*Buttons the jacket*) Push the chair back. All the way.
(BEN *picks up the chair and carries it to the far side of the room*)

BEN I thought I was bringing you two together.

WILLIE (*He shuffles over to the chair.* BEN *helps him to sit*) Put a pillow underneath. Make it two pillows. When I sit, I wanna look down on him.
(BEN *puts a pillow under* WILLIE)

BEN This is the last time. I'm never going to butt into your lives again.

WILLIE The only thing that could have made today better is if it was raining. I would love to see him apologize dripping wet. (*And then come three knocks on the door: "Knock, knock, knock"*) Aha! This is it! . . . *This* was worth getting sick for! Come on, knock again. (*Points his finger in the air, his crowning moment.* AL *knocks again*) En-terrr!

(BEN *crosses to the door and opens it.* AL LEWIS *timidly steps in, with his hat in his hand.* WILLIE *immediately drops his head to his side, closes his eyes and snores, feigning a nap*)

AL *(Whispers)* Oh, he's sleeping. I could come back later.

BEN *(Also whispers)* No, that's all right. He must be dozing. Come on in. (AL *steps in and* BEN *closes the door*) Can I take your hat?

AL No, I'd like to hold on to something, if you don't mind.
(BEN *crosses over to* WILLIE, *who is still dozing. He bends over and speaks softly in* WILLIE's *ear*)

BEN Uncle Willie. There's someone here to see you.

WILLIE *(Opens his eyes, stirs)* Heh? What?

BEN Look who's here to see you, Uncle Willie.

WILLIE *(Squints)* I don't have my glasses. Who's that?

AL It's me, Willie. Al . . . Al Lewis.

WILLIE *(Squints harder)* Al Lewis? You're so far away . . . Walk all the way over here. (AL *sheepishly makes the trek across the room with hat in hand. He squints again*) Oh, *that* Al Lewis.

AL I don't want to disturb you, Willie. I know you're resting.

WILLIE That's all right. I was just reading my telegrams from Lucille Ball and Bob Hope.

AL Oh, that's nice . . . *(Turns, looks at the vase)* Oh, look at the beautiful flowers.

WILLIE I'm throwing them out. I don't like the smell. People send them to me every day with boxes of cheap candy. They mean well.

AL (*Nods*) They certainly do . . . Well, I just came up to see how you're doing. I don't want to take up your time. I just wanted to say hello . . . So "hello"—and goodbye.
(*He starts to put on his hat to go*)

WILLIE Wait a minute. You got a few minutes before my next nap. Sit down and talk for a while.

AL You're sure it's okay?

WILLIE I'm sure you got a lot more to say than just "hello" . . . Would you like some tea?

AL I would love some.

WILLIE Go in the kitchen and make it.

BEN I've got a better idea. I'll go down and have the kitchen send up a tray. If I call room service it'll take forever.
(*He starts for the door*)

WILLIE (*To* BEN) You're going? You don't want to hear what Al has to say?

BEN I don't think it's necessary. I'll be back in ten minutes. (*At the door*) It's good to see you, Mr. Lewis . . . It's good to see the *both* of you.
(*He nods, then exits, closing the door. There is an awkward silence between the two men for a moment*)

AL *(Finally)* He's a nice boy.

WILLIE He's the best . . . Not too bright, but a good boy.

AL *(Nods)* You've got everything you need here?

WILLIE What could I need here?

AL Some books? Some magazines?

WILLIE No, I got plenty to do. I got all my fan mail to answer.

AL You get fan mail?

WILLIE Don't you?

AL I don't even get jury duty.

WILLIE Sure, plenty of people still remember . . . *(He coughs)* Excuse me.

AL You're sure it's all right for you to talk like this?

WILLIE I'm not talking. I'm just answering. *You're* talking. *(There is a long pause)* Why? Is there something special you wanted to talk about?

AL Like what?

WILLIE What do I know like what? How should I know what's on your mind? Do I know why you can't sleep at night?

AL Who said I don't sleep at night! I sleep beautifully.

WILLIE Funny, to me you look tired. A little troubled. Like a person who had something on his conscience, what do I know?

AL   I have nothing on my conscience.

WILLIE *(A pause)*   Are you sure you looked good?

AL   I have *nothing* on my conscience. The only thing I feel badly about is that you got sick.

WILLIE   Thank you. *I accept your apology!*

AL   What apology? Who apologized? I just said I'm sorry you got sick.

WILLIE   Who do you think *made* me sick?

AL   Who? *You* did, that's who! Not me. You yelled and screamed and carried on like a lunatic until you made yourself sick . . . and for that I'm sorry.

WILLIE   All right, as long as you're sorry for something.

AL   I'm also sorry that people are starving in India, but I'm not going to apologize. I didn't do it.

WILLIE   I didn't accuse you of India. I'm just saying you're responsible for making me sick, and since you've come up here to apologize, I am gentleman enough to accept it.

AL   Don't be such a gentleman, because there's nothing to accept.

WILLIE   You're the one who came up here with your hat in your hand not me.

AL   It's a twenty-five dollar hat, what was I gonna do, fold it up in my pocket?

104

WILLIE If you didn't come to apologize, why did you send me the candy and flowers?

AL I sent you candy and flowers?

WILLIE Yes. Because it was on your conscience and *that's* why you couldn't sleep at night and *that's* why you came up here with your hat in your hand to apologize, only *this* time I'm not a gentleman any more and I *don't accept the apology!* How do you like that?
    (AL *stares at* WILLIE)

AL I knew there was gonna be trouble when you said "Enter" instead of "Come in."

WILLIE There's no trouble. The trouble is over. I got what I want and now I'm happy.

AL What did you get? You got "no apology" from me, which you didn't accept.

WILLIE I don't want to discuss it any more, I just had a heart attack.
    (AL *stares at* WILLIE *silently*)

AL (*Calmly*) You know something, Willie. I don't think we get along too good.

WILLIE Well, listen, everybody has their ups and downs.

AL In forty-three years, we had maybe one "up" . . . To tell the truth, I can't take the "downs" any more.

WILLIE To be honest with you, for the first time I feel a little tired myself. In a way this heart attack was good for me. I needed the rest.

AL   So what are you going to do now?

WILLIE   Well, my nephew made me two very good of-fers today.

AL   Is that right?

WILLIE   I think I'm gonna take the second one.

AL   Are you in any condition to work again?

WILLIE   Well, it wouldn't be too strenuous . . . Mostly take it easy, maybe do a show on Saturday night, some-thing like that.

AL   Is that so? Where, in New York?

WILLIE   No, no. Out of town . . .

AL   Isn't that wonderful.

WILLIE   Well, you know me, I gotta keep busy . . . What's with you?

AL   Oh, I'm very happy. My daughter's having another baby. They're gonna need my room, and I don't want to be a burden on them. . . . So we talked it over, and I decided I'm gonna move to the Actors' Home in New Brunswick.

WILLIE   (*He sinks back onto his pillow, his head falls over to one side, and he sighs deeply*)   Ohh, God. I got the finger again.

AL   What's the matter? You all right? Why are you hold-ing your chest? You got pains?

WILLIE   Not yet. But I'm expecting.

ACT TWO

AL (*Nervously*)   Can I get you anything? Should I call the doctor?

WILLIE   It wouldn't help.

AL   It wouldn't hurt.
(*The realization that they slipped accidentally into an old vaudeville joke causes* WILLIE *to smile*)

WILLIE   "It wouldn't hurt" . . . How many times have we done that joke?

AL.   It always worked . . . Even from you I just got a laugh.

WILLIE   You're a funny man, Al . . . You're a pain in the ass, but you're a funny man.

AL   You know what your trouble was, Willie? You always took the jokes too seriously. They were just jokes. We did comedy on the stage for forty-three years, I don't think you enjoyed it once.

WILLIE   If I was there to enjoy it, I would buy a ticket.

AL   Well, maybe now you can start enjoying it . . . If you're not too busy, maybe you'll come over one day to the Actors' Home and visit me.

WILLIE   You can count on it.

AL   I feel a lot better now that I've talked to you . . . Maybe you'd like to rest now, take a nap.

WILLIE   I think so . . . Keep talking to me, I'll fall asleep.

AL (*Looks around*)   What's new in *Variety?*

WILLIE   Bernie Eisenstein died.

AL   Go on. Bernie Eisenstein? The house doctor at the Palace?

WILLIE   That was Sam Hesseltine. Bernie Eisenstein was "Ramona and Rodriguez."

AL   Jackie Aaronson was Ramona and Rodriguez. Bernie Eisenstein was the house doctor at the Palace. Sam Hesseltine was Sophie Tucker's agent.

WILLIE   Don't argue with me, I'm sick.

AL   I know. But why should I get sick too? *(The curtain starts to fall.* WILLIE *moans)* Bernie Eisenstein was the house doctor when we played for the first time with Sophie Tucker, and that's when we met Sam Hesseltine . . . Jackie Aaronson wasn't Rodriguez yet . . . He was "DeMarco and Lopez" . . . Lopez died, and DeMarco went into real estate, so Jackie became Rodriguez . . .

Curtain

Curtain Call

AL   Don't you remember Big John McCafferey? The Irishman? He owned the Biltmore Theater in Pittsburgh? And the Adams Theater in Syracuse? Always wore a two-pound diamond ring on his finger? He was the one who used to take out Mary Donatto, the cute little Italian girl from the Follies. Well, she used to go with Abe Berkowitz who was then the booker for the Orpheum circuit and Big John hated his guts because of the time when Harry Richman . . .

ABOUT THE AUTHOR

Since 1960, a Broadway season without a NEIL SIMON comedy or musical has been a rare one. During Broadway's 1966–67 season, *Barefoot in the Park, The Odd Couple, Sweet Charity,* and *Star-Spangled Girl* were all running simultaneously; in the 1970–71 season, Broadway theatergoers had their choice of *Plaza Suite, Last of the Red Hot Lovers,* and *Promises, Promises.* Mr. Simon began his writing career in television and has now distinguished himself as a playwright by producing ten successful Broadway comedies in a row. He has also written for the screen, successfully adapting *Barefoot in the Park* and *The Odd Couple,* and has also written two original screen plays, *The Out-of-Towners,* which starred Jack Lemmon and Sandy Dennis, and *The Heartbreak Kid.*

By his own analysis, "Doc" Simon has always been "that person sitting in the corner who's observing it all" for all of his forty-five years, an insight he explores in his introduction entitled "Portrait of the Artist as a Schizophrenic" written for the anthology of his plays published by Random House in 1971. That volume, *The Comedy of Neil Simon,* is a tribute to the brilliance of its author, as are the Tony Award he received as best playwright of 1965, and his selection as *Cue* magazine's Entertainer of the Year for 1972. His most recent plays are *The Prisoner of Second Avenue* and *The Sunshine Boys.*

DRAMA
SIMON
9 c.2